By

D0387167

SKINNY DIPS

60 Recipes for Dips, Spreads, Chips, and Salsas
on the Lighter Side of Delicious

SKINNY DIPS

by Diane Morgan | Photographs by Sheri Giblin

CHRONICLE BOOKS

SAN FRANCISCO

Text copyright © 2010 by Diane Morgan.
Photographs copyright © 2010 by Sheri Giblin.

Library of Congress Cataloging-in-Publication Data available.
ISBN 978-0-8118-7142-6

Manufactured in China

Designed by Alice Chau
Photo assisting by Shay Harrington
Prop styling by Christine Wolheim
Food styling by Erin Quon

10 9 8 7 6 5 4 3 2 1

Chronicle Books LLC
680 Second Street
San Francisco, CA 94107
www.chroniclebooks.com

To Greg, my soul mate, for being so supportive,
tasting everything with a discerning palate,
and never complaining about having a selection
of dips and chips and calling it dinner.

Contents

Acknowledgments

Who knew that one could develop an entire cookbook's worth of recipes and not gain weight? *Skinny Dips* has been another terrific project to work on with Chronicle Books. Months of chopping, dicing, slicing, puréeing, and pulsing has led to a collection of big-flavored, full-bodied, party-worthy dips and a crunchy selection of dippers. None of this book would have been possible without the support of my colleagues, family, and friends.

My sincerest thanks to the following:

The wonderful team at Chronicle Books, especially **Bill LeBlond** for being such a thoughtful editor, **Amy Treadwell** for years of inspiration and support, **Sarah Billingsley** for keeping my books on track, **Peter Perez** for his friendship and marketing smarts, and **David Hawk** for his responsiveness and forward-thinking ways of publicizing books.

Production Coordinator **Ben Kasman**

Managing Editor **Doug Ogan**

Photographer **Sheri Giblin**

Designer **Alice Chau**

Copyeditor **Jonathan Kauffman**

My agent, **Lisa Ekus**, for her sage advice and continuous enthusiasm, and everyone else at The Lisa Ekus Group for their dedicated support.

Andrea Slonecker, my trusted and dedicated assistant on this project; a huge thank-you for all your hard work.

Garrett Berdan, for his diet and nutrition expertise and for his careful nutritional analysis of the recipes. In addition, Garrett's thoughtful foreword for *Skinny Dips* embraces and supports my thinking on how we should eat. I just didn't know it was called "stealth health."

My enthusiastic tasters: **Harriet and Peter Watson; Roxane, Austin, Joey, and Tommy Huang; Steve and Marci Taylor; Sherry Gable; Priscilla and John Longfield; Karen Fong; Deb and Ron Adams; Summer Jamison; Ben Bettinger; Christine Belluschi; Don New; and Rafael Ornelas**.

Finally, my family—my husband, **Greg**, and my children, **Eric and Molly**—whose support and enthusiasm make my cooking and writing life possible. A huge hug and all my love.

Foreword by Garrett Berdan, RD, LD

Everyone loves a good dip. Have you ever left a cocktail party with that regretful over-full feeling, then realized you spent more time hovering over the artichoke dip than mingling? For me, this occurs every Fourth of July, when my wife's grandma makes her famous clam dip. There I am, dunking ruffled potato chips into the dip and gobbling them down, when it occurs to me that I have probably just consumed an entire day's worth of calories and saturated fat. I try to think about healthy snacking, yet at a party, I indulge.

When it's party time, most of us tend to overindulge. Mindless eating happens to the best of us. Munching, dipping, and dunking can be a huge source of calories. Many dips are made with high-fat, high-calorie ingredients—and, indeed, they taste delicious—but they should be enjoyed in smaller quantities. High-calorie snacks can add extra pounds every year.

As a registered dietitian and a chef, I teach people how to eat more healthfully and enjoy it, which is all about balancing calories from healthful foods in the appropriate portion sizes. Fundamental to healthful eating is learning how to prepare delicious food that is good for you. When food that tastes great is healthful—and you don't even know it—we call it "stealth health."

Diane Morgan's *Skinny Dips* teaches you how to make delicious dips, spreads, and dippers that are low in calories yet taste like indulgences. With this book as your guide, you can pull off a festive spread that is both easy and easy on the waistline. Diane's recipes use wholesome, naturally nutrient-rich ingredients like fresh fruit and vegetables, low-fat yogurt, fiber-filled legumes/pulses, and healthful fats from olive oil, avocados, and nuts. She calls for just enough oil, cheese, or reduced-fat sour cream to deliver fantastic flavor and richness without overdoing the calories. Her dips get a punch of flavor from spices, dry or fresh herbs, citrus juices, and vinegars. This book is full of expertly crafted recipes that taste so good, you won't know you are doing something great for your body—stealth health at its best!

Diane's *Skinny Dips* can be used for more than just snacking and parties. Incorporate these dips and spreads as a foundation of flavor when preparing low-calorie everyday meals. Dress up a salad with a bit of the Svelte Green Goddess Dip. Top a grilled chicken breast with fresh Minted Peach Salsa.

Be mindful when you dip, dunk, spread, and munch. Next time you go to a cocktail party, bring Diane's Skinny Artichoke Dip. Your friends will love it, and you can indulge free of guilt. Just don't hover.

Introduction

As a professional foodie, I'm passionate about eating—it's my life's work. I think about food constantly, and I consider chocolate an essential food group, along with good wine and great coffee. To avoid the occupational hazard of overindulging, however, I've cultivated lifelong habits of moderation and exercise that help keep me fit, trim, *and* happily fed.

Gustatory magic? Perhaps. But the real secret ingredient is that I pay attention to what I eat on so many levels, tasting for an amazing flavor, a delightful texture, comfort food to satisfy a longing, a luscious sweet sensation, an exotic new ingredient that excites my palate, or even a feel-good food when I'm sick. Perhaps most important, I eat slowly to savor these foods that mean so much to me, and I know when I'm full and sated. No self-imposed deprivation here. Just a sensible, thoughtful approach to eating.

I try to bring that consciousness to all the recipes I develop. It is so easy to add a lot of butter and cream to a dish and make it taste great. It is harder—but more satisfying—to develop recipes that do without butter and cream and to discover the amazing richness of flavor that can be found in many low-calorie foods.

In writing *Skinny Dips*, I gave myself a series of challenges. Would it be possible to develop a book full of healthful, calorie-conscious, big-flavored, party-worthy dips and, in addition, create irresistibly crispy dippers? Beyond that, could I serve these dips to unsuspecting guests and have them convinced they were indulging in fabulous party fare, calories be damned? The results: yes and yes!

Plan the Right Party

Entertaining any time of year, whether large or small, casual or formal, inside or outdoors, involves nibbles and nosh—starters to get the party rolling. With a drink in one hand, guests have the other hand free for dunking, scooping, slathering, and spreading all those wonderful concoctions the host has made.

With *Skinny Dips* in hand, you can peruse more than sixty delectable dips and tempting chips, select the foods that fit the mood of your party, and learn creative ways to go light on the fat without sacrificing big flavor. (Just one example: The recipes in the final chapter for baked chips that are as crisp and addictive as the fried alternatives.)

Skinny Dips is a book for the cook in the know and the guests who don't really need to know. These dips, spreads, and chips can be at the center of a convivial "stealth health" affair. Super Bowl Sunday doesn't have to be a calorie-fest when great salsas (which aren't fattening to begin with), baked chips, and skinny guacamoles can replace the classic calorie-laden recipes. When the panic of swimsuit season hits, your guests will be better served by a summer entertaining menu that includes light dips and garden-fresh crudités.

With everyone pressed for time, entertaining can feel overwhelming. However, making dips is easy on the host—no fussy hors d'oeuvres to assemble and delicately garnish. Rarely are dips last-minute affairs requiring timing and finesse. Most dips are stirred, whipped, or whirled and then scooped into a serving bowl. While the novice cook might feel more relaxed just making a dip and opening a bag or two of store-bought chips, the cook looking for fun and play in the kitchen can make dips and bake crisps and chips. It's all in *Skinny Dips*!

About these Recipes

Every chapter is packed with contemporary recipes featuring global flavors and tastes—all with a light touch. In addition, the vegetable and herb dips are a gardener's delight. If you have an abundance of zucchini/courgettes, make the Turkish Zucchini & Walnut Dip (page 36), or when you don't know what to do with the overflowing bag of eggplants/aubergines, make the Indian Tomato-Eggplant Dip on page 29. Don't give away your bumper crop of tomatoes—have a late summer party and make Skinny Tomato Salsa (page 46).

To help you plan, I have included a "Dip Do-Ahead" or "Dipper Do-Ahead" with each recipe. You'll know how far in advance a recipe can be made, how to store it, and how to reheat the dip if that's what's called for. In addition, I have given you my favorite chip and dip pairings for each recipe. Finally, every dip recipe includes nutritional analysis. For special dietary considerations, such as low-salt or low-cholesterol diets, you'll have the facts right at hand.

So go ahead and throw a terrific party with great dips and chips, great conversation, and great fun!

Healthful Ingredient Glossary

Ancho Chiles

The dried form of a poblano pepper is called an ancho chile. *Ancho* means "wide" in Spanish, which accurately describes the shape of this large, heart-shaped pepper. Deep reddish brown to near black in color, anchos are sweeter than other dried chiles, and their heat ranges from mild to strong. They are often ground into a powder; whole anchos can be soaked in water for 30 to 45 minutes to rehydrate before use.

Artichokes

Artichokes, canned or fresh, are the perfect food for lightening up your diet. I call them a "free food," because they can be eaten to your heart's content with zero guilt. An entire 13.75-oz/390-g can of artichokes has about 100 calories. In my dip recipes, I call for canned artichokes—be sure to purchase them in brine or water rather than in oil or marinated. If you are steaming artichokes for use as a skinny dipper (see page 127), purchase whole, fresh artichokes with tight heads that feel heavy for their size and have little to no browning on the tips of the leaves. In general, smaller artichokes will have more tender flesh, but the more round a choke is, the larger its meaty heart.

Avocados

This tropical fruit, which can be either round or pear-shaped, has a creamy, buttery flesh. Though avocados have an exceptionally high fat content for a fruit, two-thirds of the fat is the "good" mono-unsaturated variety that does not raise blood cholesterol levels. Eaten in moderation, avocados are considered one of the top ten nutrient-dense foods—powerhouses of vitamins, minerals, and phytonutrients. Generally, you'll see two types of avocados in the market. Hass avocados have a pebbly texture and purplish-black skin, while Fuerte avocados have a smooth and shiny bright-green skin. I prefer the Hass variety because the flesh is richer and fuller flavored. Look for avocados that are unblemished and heavy for their size. Ripe avocados yield to gentle pressure but shouldn't be soft. If you purchase unripe fruits, let them ripen at room temperature; to speed the process, put them in a paper bag. Once avocados are cut, the flesh starts to discolor. For guacamole, adding citrus juice helps to prevent discoloration, but the longer the guacamole sits, the browner it turns. Guacamole is at its best when served within a few hours of being made.

Cheese

In this book, I work with everything from fat-free feta to full-fat blue cheese. Used in smaller doses, varieties like blue cheese and fresh goat's milk cheese add a lot of flavor without tipping the scale, calorically speaking. Grated Parmigiano-Reggiano packs a sweet and nutty punch, with only 20 calories and 1.5 grams of fat per tablespoon. Reduced-fat cheese comes in a variety of styles, forms, and flavors. Pre-shredded cheeses like some Mexican blends and brands of mozzarella are often made with 2% milk, which lightens the fat and calories. For Cheddar, I buy bricks of the one-third-less-fat variety (sometimes labeled "reduced fat"), which melts well and maintains a sharp flavor. In general, stay away from the fat-free cheeses—they don't melt well, and the flavor and texture resemble plastic. One exception is fat-free feta, which works quite well in the Baked Feta Spinach Dip on page 71.

Chipotle Chiles in Adobo

Chipotle chiles are smoke-dried jalapeños that are canned in *adobo* (a sauce made from ground chiles, herbs, and vinegar). Look for them stocked with other Mexican foods in supermarkets.

Chorizo

Chorizo is a Mexican sausage made from highly seasoned, coarsely ground pork. Garlic and powdered red chiles dominate its flavor. Chorizo is sold either in links or in bulk. For the recipes in this book, buy bulk chorizo if available; otherwise, remove the casing from link sausages before browning. Look for Mexican chorizo, which is made from fresh pork. Spanish chorizo, though equally delicious, is made from smoked pork; it is not the type I refer to when I call for "chorizo" in the dip recipes. Though chorizo is not a low-fat ingredient, in small quantities it packs a lot of flavor, which is why I use it in moderation.

Cream Cheese

Bar-style, one-third-less-fat cream cheese (also known as Neufchâtel) is available in any supermarket. Out of all of the "light" dairy products used in this book, low-fat cream cheese tastes closest to the full-fat version. It's my bet that no one will be able to tell the difference. Two tablespoons of light cream cheese contains 70 calories and 5 grams of fat, compared to 90 calories and 9 grams of fat in the regular version. It may be tempting to try the fat-free version, but I advise against it—the flavor is quite artificial and the texture not nearly as creamy. Whipped cream cheese is also available and contributes fewer calories and fat per tablespoon due to the addition of air in the whipping process. The texture is lighter and fluffier, which is the desired result for the dip in which it is used.

Lavash

Lavash, lavosh, or lahvosh is a gigantic, paper-thin, blistery, tortilla-like flatbread common throughout Armenia, Turkey, and Iran. It comes in various sizes ranging from 6 in/15 cm to 14 in/35.5 cm in diameter. A soft version is sold, but I prefer to buy the large cracker-style lavash because I can serve it crisp or softened. To soften a piece of the crisp bread, thoroughly wet both sides by holding it under cold running water. Wrap the lavash with dampened, large, clean cotton kitchen towels for about 45 minutes. Sprinkle with additional water and wrap for a little longer if not completely pliable.

Mayonnaise

Reduced-fat mayonnaise has less than half of the calories and about a third of the fat of regular mayonnaise. Calorically speaking, you get a huge bang for your buck—without sacrificing flavor and texture—just by making this substitution. All the recipes in this book were tested with the Best Foods (also known as Hellmann's) brand of "light" mayonnaise.

Potato Chips and Other Store-Bought Chips

Almost every potato chip producer now makes baked chips. Kettle Brand makes a particularly good "lightly salted" version that is super-crunchy and sturdy for scooping. In comparison to fried potato chips, the baked variety has about one-fifth the fat content. That's a significant savings. I can eat 20 baked chips and consume only 120 calories! As far as baking potato chips at home—honestly, why go through the hassle when there are so many great options at the supermarket? Also look for baked rice chips and pretzel chips at the store—they, too, make excellent skinny dippers. The same is not true for pita chips and bagel chips, however. Store-bought packages always have many broken chips, and besides, these chips are easy to make at home (pages 133–138) with terrific results.

Roasted-Garlic Olive Oil

Supermarkets are giving over more shelf space to flavored olive oils. It's fun to experiment with different oils, especially because a little goes a long way, packing a flavor punch without delivering a caloric overload, too. Roasted-garlic olive oil adds a subtle garlic flavor to several of the dips in the book. Use extra-virgin olive oil if you can't find garlic-infused oil.

Salt

I keep several types of salt in my kitchen. Within easy reach of my stove and prep counter are a bowl of kosher salt and another filled with fine sea salt. I buy Diamond Crystal kosher salt, in the red box, which is available at specialty-food shops and many supermarkets. Kosher salt has a bright, salty taste and big, crunchy flakes that are nice for sprinkling on finished dishes. The sea salt I use comes from the Mediterranean. In cooking, I like to use extra-fine sea salt because it dissolves quickly and has a clean, delicate taste. I never use ordinary table salt because it includes an anticaking agent that leaves a chemical aftertaste.

Sour Cream

Most dairy companies that make sour cream also produce a reduced-fat version. It's creamy, not remarkably different in taste when mixed into a skinny dip, and a calorie cutter. There are about 40 calories and 2.5 grams of fat in two tablespoons of reduced-fat sour cream—that's nearly 50 percent less fat and calories compared to the full-fat variety.

Tahini

This sesame seed paste is typically available in Middle Eastern and natural-foods stores and in the health-food sections of many supermarkets. As with natural peanut butter, when you open a can or jar of tahini, you will find a layer of oil separated on top, which simply needs to be stirred back into the ground paste before using. Store leftover tahini in the refrigerator; when tightly sealed, it seems to keep indefinitely.

Yogurt

I like to use low-fat plain yogurt in Middle Eastern and Indian dips such as the Butternut Squash Bharit on page 22. Low-fat yogurt adds a silky texture and a tart undertone with very little fat and calories. Avoid fat-free yogurt, as it tends to be watery and won't contribute the smooth mouthfeel that low-fat varieties do. Yogurt is a nutrient-rich food—a complete protein full of calcium, vitamins B_6 and B_{12}, and riboflavin, as well as probiotics that aid digestion.

Skinny Dip Tips and Techniques

Using the Food Processor

Beyond a sharp chef's knife and paring knife, a cutting board, and a couple of sauté pans, there is only one piece of equipment you will need in order to successfully make most of the dips in this book: a food processor. Honestly, in order to pulse, process, and purée to achieve the desired consistency of these dips, you simply need its whirling action. Neither a blender nor a mixer gives you the same magical smoothness for a bean dip, or the right chunkiness when you just want to pulse-chop ingredients (for example, for the Artichoke Pesto on page 35). Fortunately, this time-saving device comes in many makes and models and is often discounted at big-box stores, department stores, and cookware shops. You don't need a giant machine. In fact, I would discourage you from buying anything beyond a standard 11-cup/3-L model. I have always owned this size of food processor, and it meets all of my preparation needs.

Handling and Cutting Fresh Chiles

Buy disposable surgical gloves at the pharmacy and wear them when you work with chiles. They will keep the caustic compound (capsaicin) naturally present in chiles from irritating your skin—and from burning your eyes if you accidentally rub them after handling chiles.

Roasting Fresh Chiles and Bell Peppers/Capsicums

There are several ways to easily roast and char the skins of chiles or bell peppers/capsicums:

UNDER THE BROILER/GRILL: Set an oven rack 5 to 6 in/12.5 to 15 cm from the heat source and turn on the broiler/grill. Place whole peppers/capsicums on a rimmed baking sheet/tray and broil/grill, turning frequently, until the skin blisters and chars on all sides. Remove from the oven, enclose in damp paper towels/absorbent paper, and seal in a plastic bag for 7 to 10 minutes. Use the paper to rub off the skin. Cut the peppers/capsicums in half and discard the cores, seeds, and ribs. Then prepare according to recipe directions.

ON THE GRILL/BARBECUE: Prepare a hot fire in a charcoal grill/barbecue or turn a gas grill/barbecue to high. Grill the peppers/capsicums, turning frequently, until the skin blisters and chars on all sides. Remove from the heat and proceed as directed.

USING A GAS BURNER: Set the grilling grate from a small hibachi or a 9-in/ 23-cm round cooling rack (preferably an old one that you don't care that much about) directly on the burner grate. Turn the burner to medium or medium-high, place the peppers/capsicums on the rack, and roast, turning frequently, until the skin blisters and chars on all sides. Remove from the heat and proceed as directed.

Use roasted peppers/capsicums or chiles immediately, or place in a covered container and refrigerate for up to 3 days. They will keep longer if covered with a good-quality olive oil and stored in the refrigerator. They can also be stored in the freezer, though there is some loss of quality in their texture.

Store-bought roasted peppers/capsicums are a good substitute when you are in a hurry or just don't want to bother roasting your own. Roasted red peppers packed in a light vinegar brine are sold in jars at specialty-food shops or supermarkets. Once opened, store any leftovers in the refrigerator, making sure they are immersed in the brine. They will keep for a couple of weeks.

Roasting Garlic

Roasted garlic is a wonderful condiment to have on hand. I mash it with a little olive oil and spread it on bruschetta. I also add it to salad dressings, tomato sauces, and potato gratins. And, as you'll see, adding roasted garlic to dips contributes a distinctive mellow garlic flavor without the bite of fresh garlic.

Here's an easy recipe: Preheat the oven to 375°F/190°C/gas 5. Peel the loose, papery outer layers of skin off 2 heads of garlic and trim any roots from the bottom. Cut off enough of the top of the garlic heads to expose the cloves. Place each head of garlic on a sheet of foil large enough to completely enclose it, with a little extra foil left over. Drizzle each head with 1 teaspoon of olive oil and sprinkle with a little salt. Wrap the foil tightly around the bulbs, twisting it closed at the top. Place on a small rimmed baking sheet/tray and roast until the garlic feels soft when pierced with a knife, about 45 minutes. Open the foil packages and bake until the garlic cloves begin to pop from their skins and brown, about 15 minutes longer. Remove from the oven and let cool. Squeeze the roasted garlic cloves from the skins. Store, tightly covered, in the refrigerator, for up to 3 weeks.

17

Toasting Nuts and Seeds

Toasting pine nuts, almonds, walnuts, pecans, hazelnuts, cashews, and pumpkin seeds brings out their fullest, richest flavor. Place the nuts or seeds in a single layer on a rimmed baking sheet/tray and bake in a preheated 350°F/180°C/gas 4 oven until lightly browned, 5 to 10 minutes, depending on the nut or seed. Alternatively, nuts and seeds can be browned in a microwave. Place in a single layer on a microwave-safe plate, and microwave on high power for 2 to 3 minutes, or until lightly browned, stirring once or twice while they are toasting. Watch carefully that they don't burn.

Toasting Spices

Dry-roasting whole spices in a frying pan and then grinding them maximizes their flavor and scent. Place a small, heavy frying pan, preferably cast iron, over high heat. Add the spices to the pan and, stirring constantly, toast until fragrant and lightly browned, about 2 minutes. Transfer to a plate to cool. The spices can then be ground in a blender or spice grinder or with a mortar and pestle. Blend or grind to a powder. Lacking any of the aforementioned tools, place the toasted spices in a heavy lock-top plastic bag and pound them with a rolling pin or the bottom of a small, heavy saucepan.

Zesting Citrus

Using a handheld gadget called a zester, you can easily remove the zest (the colored part of the rind, without the white pith underneath) from a lemon, lime, orange, or grapefruit by drawing the zester across the skin of the fruit. My favorite tool for removing zest is a Microplane grater, available at kitchen shops everywhere. I prefer the texture of the zest a Microplane yields, and with a "tap-tap-tap" of the tool against a cutting board, the zest falls right off, ready to scoop up and measure. Buy a zester with a handle for easier use. Be sure to wash and dry any citrus before zesting to remove any sprays remaining on the fruit.

Party Planning Tips

Entertaining is all about preparing good food and drink, setting the mood, and making your guests feel comfortable. It is also about throwing a party that fits your lifestyle, budget, energy level, and time frame. Entertaining is supposed to be fun for all.

Dips and chips are easy on the host. There are no fussy hors d'oeuvres to assemble and garnish, no last-minute sautéing, baking, or broiling to worry about. Moreover, being highly skilled in the kitchen is not required. That said, a few tips and organizational suggestions will help you bring a relaxed, can-do spirit to the hassles and triumphs of entertaining, whether you are throwing a holiday open house, celebrating a special occasion, gathering for a bowl day bash, or lighting the grill for a backyard barbecue.

Planning and Organization

STEP ONE: MAKE A FEW LISTS. Create a guest list, plan a menu, write a shopping list, and list the errands you need to run to prepare for the event. Most important, write a day-by-day schedule to organize your time. I realize all this documenting sounds like war-room strategizing for a major attack, but stress-free entertaining requires a plan.

STEP TWO: STOCK YOUR PANTRY. Keep pantry staples on hand for spur-of-the-moment entertaining. Just think: With canned beans on the shelf, along with olive oil, garlic, and dried herbs, you can whip together a dip in no time. Keeping a selection of chips and crackers, and even simple crudités, on hand means party food is ready to go. I reach for canned tuna, frozen spinach and edamame, a chunk of Parmesan cheese, olives, capers, and mayonnaise without thinking twice—they are my essential building blocks for easy entertaining.

STEP THREE: KEEP IT SIMPLE. Casual entertaining centered around dips and chips does not require you, the host, to muster up a battery of equipment, dishes, and glassware. The critical piece of equipment is a food processor (see page 16). The clever host doesn't need a cabinet full of dishes, either, to lay out your spread. Spoon dips into bowls or shallow baking dishes. Set them on complementary plates or in baskets lined with fun paper or cloth napkins, then nestle chips around. Think creatively—I've used a curled red cabbage leaf to hold a dip and hollowed out half a pineapple to spoon a tropical salsa into.

STEP FOUR: HAVE FUN. The essence of hosting a memorable evening is simply to gather friends and family around the table to laugh and enjoy being together, and that includes the host, too!

CHAPTER 1

Vegetable and Herb Dips

Colorful, farm-fresh vegetables packed with vitamins and minerals are powerhouse foods. Not only do vegetables give us more energy and help protect against disease, eating them gives us a nutritious way to take off pounds. Vegetables fill us up without packing on the calories. Turned into dips, vegetables can be even more of a "stealth health" indulgence! A quarter cup/60 ml of Butternut Squash Bharit contains only 60 calories, with a mere 3 grams of fat. The same amount of Baba Ghanoush has only 38 calories and less than 3 grams of fat. Shop the farmers' market or walk through your grocer's produce aisle, then throw a party with a rainbow of seasonal, deliciously fresh, and healthful dips.

SERVING SIZE

1/4

cup
(60 ml)

CALORIES	60
FAT	3 g
SAT	1.5 g
MONO	1.2 g
POLY	0.2 g
PROTEIN	2 g
CARB	8 g
FIBER	0 g
CHOL	5 mg
IRON	0.5 mg
SODIUM	216 mg
CALC	74 mg

Butternut Squash Bharit

I make this dip in the fall and winter, when butternut squash is local and abundant at the farmers' market. This roasted and mashed Indian dip would be delightful at Thanksgiving or for any wintertime party.

1 small BUTTERNUT SQUASH (about 1 lb/455 g), cut in half
    lengthwise and seeded

2 tsp EXTRA-VIRGIN OLIVE OIL

1 tbsp UNSALTED BUTTER

1 tbsp CURRY POWDER

1 cup/240 ml LOW-FAT PLAIN YOGURT

1 tbsp seeded and minced SERRANO CHILE (see page 16)

1 tbsp minced CILANTRO/FRESH CORIANDER LEAVES

1 1/2 tsp KOSHER OR SEA SALT

2 sprigs CILANTRO/FRESH CORIANDER for garnish

SKINNY DIPPERS: Roasted Cauliflower, Baked Pita Chips, Parmesan-Crusted Pita Chips, Herbed Cheddar Cheese Straws, vegetable chips

1. Preheat the oven to 350°F/180°C/gas 4. Brush the flesh of the squash with the olive oil and arrange, cut-side down, on a rimmed baking sheet/tray. Roast until very tender when pierced, about 40 minutes. Set aside until cool enough to handle, about 20 minutes.

2. In a small nonstick frying pan over medium heat, melt the butter. Add the curry powder and stir, allowing the spices to cook until fragrant, about 10 seconds. Remove from the heat.

3. Use a spoon to scrape out the flesh of the squash and put it in the workbowl of a food processor fitted with the metal blade. Discard the skins. Purée until smooth. Add the curried butter and pulse to incorporate. Add the yogurt, chile, minced cilantro/fresh coriander, and salt. Process to combine, then taste and adjust the seasoning. Transfer to a serving bowl, garnish with the cilantro sprigs, and serve immediately.

DIP DO-AHEAD: This dip can be prepared up to 3 days in advance. Cover and refrigerate. Rewarm in a microwave or on the stovetop in a double boiler just before serving.

Baba Ghanoush

Grilling gives this dip its distinctive flavor. Roasting the eggplant in the oven will also work, but the results will differ slightly. For this dip, I use the globe variety. Look for ones that are firm, with glossy skin.

2 medium EGGPLANTS/AUBERGINES (about 2 lbs/910 g total)

2 large cloves GARLIC

1 JALAPEÑO CHILE, quartered and seeded (see page 16)

½ cup/25 g lightly packed FRESH FLAT-LEAF PARSLEY leaves

2 tbsp TAHINI

2 tbsp FRESH LEMON JUICE

2 tbsp LOW-FAT PLAIN YOGURT

1 tsp KOSHER OR SEA SALT

FRESHLY GROUND PEPPER

SKINNY DIPPERS: Crudités, Bruschetta, Crostini, Baked Pita Chips, Spice-Coated Pita Chips, lavash

1. Prepare a medium-low fire in a charcoal grill/barbecue, or preheat a gas or electric grill/barbecue on medium-low. Pierce the skin of the eggplants/aubergines in several places. Grill/barbecue, covered, directly over the fire, turning every 10 minutes. Grill until completely tender when pierced, about 30 minutes. Remove from the grill and let cool for about 10 minutes. (Alternatively, you can roast the pierced eggplants/aubergines on a rimmed baking sheet/tray in a preheated 375°F/190°C/gas 5 oven until very tender, about 45 minutes.)

2. In the workbowl of a food processor fitted with the metal blade, process the garlic, jalapeño, and parsley until minced. Halve the eggplants/aubergines lengthwise and scoop the flesh into the food processor. Discard the skins. Add the tahini, lemon juice, yogurt, salt, and a few grinds of pepper. Process the mixture just until combined. Taste and adjust the seasoning. Transfer to a serving bowl and serve immediately.

DIP DO-AHEAD: This dip can be prepared up to 2 days in advance. Cover and refrigerate. Remove from the refrigerator 45 minutes before serving. Serve the dip at room temperature.

MAKES
about

2

cups
(480 ml)

SERVING SIZE

2

tbsp

CALORIES	19
FAT	1.1 g
SAT	0.2 g
MONO	0.4 g
POLY	0.5 g
PROTEIN	1 g
CARB	2 g
FIBER	1 g
CHOL	0 mg
IRON	0.3 mg
SODIUM	77 mg
CALC	16 mg

SERVING SIZE

2

tbsp

CALORIES	62
FAT	4.9 g
SAT	0.5 g
MONO	3.2 g
POLY	1 g
PROTEIN	2 g
CARB	4 g
FIBER	1 g
CHOL	0 mg
IRON	0.7 mg
SODIUM	97 mg
CALC	21 mg

Light Romesco Spread

It may seem a bit brazen to take a classic Catalan sauce, remove most of the olive oil to lighten it up, and declare it addictively delicious. But that's what my dinner-party guests called this romesco sauce when I served it with poached shrimp and roasted cauliflower.

2 medium ANCHO CHILES

4 large cloves GARLIC

1 large ROASTED RED BELL PEPPER/CAPSICUM (see page 16), coarsely chopped

1 cup/115 g BLANCHED ALMONDS, toasted (see page 18)

1 can (14.5 oz/415 g) DICED TOMATOES, drained

2 tbsp RED WINE VINEGAR

1¼ tsp KOSHER OR SEA SALT

1 tsp PIMENTÓN (Spanish smoked paprika)

¼ tsp SUGAR

⅛ tsp CAYENNE PEPPER

3 tbsp EXTRA-VIRGIN OLIVE OIL

SKINNY DIPPERS: Roasted Cauliflower, Poached Shrimp, Roasted Fingerling Potatoes, Crostini, Herbed Cheddar Cheese Straws

1. To prepare the ancho chiles, remove the stems and seeds, then soak the chiles in hot water to cover until softened, about 45 minutes. Drain well and tear into small pieces.

2. In the workbowl of a food processor fitted with the metal blade, process the garlic until finely minced. Add the chiles, roasted pepper/capsicum, almonds, tomatoes, vinegar, salt, pimentón, sugar, and cayenne. Pulse until uniformly minced, scraping down the sides of the bowl once or twice. With the machine running, slowly add the olive oil and process just until combined. Taste and adjust the seasoning. Transfer to a serving bowl, cover, and set aside for at least 1 hour to allow the flavors to meld.

DIP DO-AHEAD: This sauce keeps, tightly covered, in the refrigerator for up to 3 months. Remove from the refrigerator 45 minutes before serving. Serve at room temperature.

MAKES

2¹/₂

cups
(600 ml)

SERVING SIZE

2

tbsp

CALORIES	34
FAT	1.9 g
SAT	0.4 g
MONO	0.7 g
POLY	0.3 g
PROTEIN	1 g
CARB	4 g
FIBER	1 g
CHOL	2 mg
IRON	0.3 mg
SODIUM	209 mg
CALC	35 mg

Curried Cauliflower Dip

When I was developing the vegetable dips for this book, I thought about the seductive aromas and flavors that come from popping black mustard seeds in a frying pan and sautéing onions with curry powder, and I knew this would make a great base for a low-calorie dip. If you think cauliflower is an odd vegetable to use for a dip, wait till you taste this one, in which it's mashed together with yogurt, spices, and pretty flecks of parsley. Get ready for the compliments.

1 head CAULIFLOWER (about 1½ lb/680 g), broken into florets, and florets halved

1¾ tsp KOSHER OR SEA SALT

1 tbsp CANOLA OIL

1 tsp BLACK MUSTARD SEEDS

1 medium YELLOW ONION, finely diced

1 tbsp CURRY POWDER

1 tbsp SUGAR

1 cup/240 ml LOW-FAT PLAIN YOGURT

¼ cup/60 ml REDUCED-FAT SOUR CREAM

⅓ cup/ 17 g coarsely chopped FRESH FLAT-LEAF PARSLEY

Dash of FRESHLY GROUND NUTMEG

Dash of CAYENNE PEPPER

FRESHLY GROUND PEPPER

SKINNY DIPPERS: Crudités, Crostini, Baked Pita Chips, Baked Bagel Chips, Baked Tortilla Chips, Seeded Tortilla Chips, taro root or yuca chips

1. Fill a 4-qt/4-L saucepan with 2 in/5 cm of water and bring to a boil over high heat. Add the cauliflower and ¼ teaspoon of the salt. Partially cover the pan, adjust the heat so the water simmers, and cook the cauliflower until tender when pierced with a fork, about 10 minutes. Drain completely and transfer to a bowl.

2. In a small sauté pan over medium heat, warm the oil and swirl to coat the pan. Add the black mustard seeds, cover the pan, and cook until the seeds have stopped popping, about 30 seconds. Add the onion and sauté until soft and translucent, about 5 minutes. Add the curry powder, the remaining 1½ tsp of salt, and the sugar, and stir constantly until the curry is fragrant, 1 to 2 minutes longer. Remove from the heat.

3. Use a fork to mash the cauliflower into very small pieces. Add the curry mixture and stir to combine. Using a rubber spatula, stir in the yogurt, sour cream, parsley, nutmeg, cayenne, and a few grinds of pepper. Taste and adjust the seasoning. Transfer to a serving bowl and serve immediately.

DIP DO-AHEAD: This dip can be prepared up to 2 days in advance. Cover and refrigerate. Remove from the refrigerator 45 minutes before serving. Serve the dip at room temperature.

CALORIES	46
FAT	3 g
SAT	1.1 g
MONO	0.6 g
POLY	0.1 g
PROTEIN	2 g
CARB	3 g
FIBER	1 g
CHOL	6 mg
IRON	0.2 mg
SODIUM	140 mg
CALC	49 mg

Skinny Artichoke Dip

When it comes to calories, artichokes are almost "free"—a half cup has only 35 calories. As cheeses go, Parmesan is on the light side.

1 large SHALLOT, halved

2 cans (13.75 oz/390 g each) ARTICHOKE HEARTS packed in water, well drained

½ cup/120 ml REDUCED-FAT MAYONNAISE

½ cup/120 ml REDUCED-FAT SOUR CREAM

1 tbsp FRESH LEMON JUICE

1 cup/115 g freshly grated PARMESAN CHEESE, preferably Parmigiano-Reggiano

½ tsp KOSHER OR SEA SALT

FRESHLY GROUND PEPPER

⅓ cup/40 g unseasoned dry BREAD CRUMBS

1½ tsp finely minced FRESH OREGANO

2 tsp EXTRA-VIRGIN OLIVE OIL

SKINNY DIPPERS: Crostini, Baked Pita Chips, Parmesan-Crusted Pita Chips, Baked Bagel Chips, Baked Wonton Crisps

1. In the workbowl of a food processor fitted with the metal blade, pulse the shallot and artichoke hearts until coarsely chopped. In a medium bowl, combine the mayonnaise, sour cream, lemon juice, Parmesan, and salt. Add the chopped shallots and artichokes. Season with pepper. Transfer to a buttered 1½-qt/1.4-L baking dish.

2. In a small bowl, combine the bread crumbs, oregano, and olive oil, mixing until the oil evenly coats the bread crumbs.

3. Position a rack in the upper third of the oven and preheat the oven to 400°F/200°C/gas 6. Just before baking, sprinkle the bread-crumb mixture on top of the artichoke dip. Bake until the dip bubbles at the edges, 20 to 25 minutes. Serve hot.

DIP DO-AHEAD: The dip, without the bread-crumb topping, can be prepared, covered, and refrigerated up to 2 days in advance. Remove from the refrigerator 40 minutes before baking.

Indian Tomato-Eggplant Dip

Friends couldn't stop eating this dip when I served it with cocktails before a dinner party. I have to agree—it is completely addictive. This sultry dip reminds me of the complex spicing I encountered during a culinary tour of India. The ingredients meld into a coarse but velvety, deeply burnished purée with tiny flecks of green from the cilantro/ fresh coriander. It does not taste strongly of either tomato or eggplant/ aubergine, but rather a lovely blending of these fruits. Honestly, you can hover over this dip, because it is low in calories and nearly fat free.

1 EGGPLANT/AUBERGINE (about 1¼ lb/570 g), halved lengthwise

1 tbsp CANOLA OIL

1 cup/135 g finely minced WALLA WALLA OR OTHER SWEET ONION

1 tsp minced GARLIC

1 tsp minced GINGER

¾ cup/145 g finely chopped PLUM TOMATOES

2 tsp TOMATO PASTE/TOMATO PURÉE

2 to 3 tsp CHILI POWDER

2 tsp KOSHER OR SEA SALT

½ tsp GROUND CUMIN

½ tsp GROUND CORIANDER

½ tsp TURMERIC

2 tbsp finely minced CILANTRO/FRESH CORIANDER LEAVES

¼ cup/60 ml WATER

1 tbsp LOW-FAT PLAIN YOGURT

SKINNY DIPPERS: Roasted Cauliflower, Crudités, Baked Pita Chips, Crostini, Bruschetta, baked potato chips

CONTINUED »

SERVING SIZE

2

tbsp

CALORIES	30
FAT	2.1 g
SAT	0.1 g
MONO	0.8 g
POLY	0.4 g
PROTEIN	0 g
CARB	3 g
FIBER	1 g
CHOL	0 mg
IRON	0.3 mg
SODIUM	211 mg
CALC	10 mg

1. Preheat the oven to 500°F/260°C/gas 10. Arrange the egg-plant/aubergine halves, flesh-side down, on a rimmed baking sheet/tray. Roast until very soft and tender when the flesh is pierced with a fork, 15 to 20 minutes. Set aside to cool for 10 minutes. Using a paring knife, peel back the skin and discard. Transfer the cooked flesh to a cutting board and finely chop.

2. In a 10-in/25-cm frying pan, preferably nonstick, heat the oil over medium heat and swirl to coat the pan. Add the onion and sauté until soft but not brown, 5 to 7 minutes. Add the garlic and ginger and sauté until fragrant, about 1 minute. Add the tomatoes and tomato paste/tomato purée. Sauté, stirring frequently, until the tomatoes soften, about 3 minutes. Add the chili powder, salt, cumin, coriander, and turmeric. Sauté to incorporate the spices, 1 minute longer. Add the roasted eggplant/aubergine and sauté, stirring constantly, until the mixture is well combined, about 2 minutes. Adjust the heat to medium-low and gently stir in 1 tbsp of the cilantro/fresh coriander and the water and yogurt. Cook over low heat until slightly thickened and a good dipping consistency, about 5 minutes. Transfer to a serving bowl, garnish with the remaining 1 tbsp cilantro/fresh coriander, and serve immediately.

DIP DO-AHEAD: This dip can be prepared up to 3 days in advance. Cover and refrigerate. Remove from the refrigerator 45 minutes before serving. Serve the dip at room temperature.

SERVING SIZE

2

tbsp

CALORIES	61
FAT	5.1 g
SAT	1.7 g
MONO	0.6 g
POLY	0.1 g
PROTEIN	1 g
CARB	3 g
FIBER	0 g
CHOL	8 mg
IRON	0.3 mg
SODIUM	195 mg
CALC	28 mg

Svelte Green Goddess Dip

Those of you with an herb garden will find this summertime dip easy to make—the recipe turns a bundle of fresh-clipped herbs into a delicate green, creamy sauce. The perfect dippers to go with it are garden-fresh vegetables such as asparagus, carrots, radishes, and cucumber.

2 oil-packed ANCHOVY FILLETS, rinsed and blotted dry

1 large clove GARLIC, smashed

2 GREEN/SPRING ONIONS, including 3 in/7.5 cm of the green tops, cut into ½-in/12-mm lengths

¼ cup/13 g lightly packed FRESH FLAT-LEAF PARSLEY leaves

¼ cup/15 g lightly packed CILANTRO/FRESH CORIANDER LEAVES

¼ cup/12 g chopped FRESH DILL

2 tbsp coarsely chopped FRESH TARRAGON LEAVES

6 large FRESH BASIL LEAVES, torn into small pieces

2 tbsp WHITE WINE VINEGAR

1 tsp KOSHER OR SEA SALT

1 tsp SUGAR

⅛ tsp FRESHLY GROUND PEPPER

¾ cup/180 ml REDUCED-FAT SOUR CREAM

½ cup/120 ml REDUCED-FAT MAYONNAISE

SKINNY DIPPERS: Crudités, Baked Pita Chips, Baked Wonton Crisps, Baked Bagel Chips, Steamed Baby Artichokes

In the workbowl of a food processor fitted with the metal blade, process the anchovies, garlic, green/spring onions, parsley, cilantro/fresh coriander, dill, tarragon, basil, vinegar, salt, sugar, and pepper until finely chopped. Stop the machine once or twice to scrape down the sides of the bowl with a rubber spatula. Add the sour cream and mayonnaise. Process until smooth. Transfer to a serving bowl, cover, and refrigerate for at least 1 hour to allow the flavors to meld.

DIP DO-AHEAD: This dip can be prepared up to 2 days in advance. Cover and refrigerate. Remove from the refrigerator 10 minutes before serving.

SERVING SIZE

1

tbsp

CALORIES	58
FAT	5.1 g
SAT	1 g
MONO	3 g
POLY	1 g
PROTEIN	2 g
CARB	2 g
FIBER	1 g
CHOL	2 mg
IRON	0.3 mg
SODIUM	57 mg
CALC	31 mg

Pistachio Pesto

The big flavor of this pesto helps you eat "skinny" while preserving great taste. Eating little bites of luscious foods is the way I limit my indulgences, and this decadent pesto is a perfect example. Altogether, the pistachios, Parmesan, and olive oil in the recipe add up to about 1,400 calories; however, no one person is going to eat the entire batch of pesto. The recipe makes 1½ cups/360 ml of pesto, or 24 tablespoons. Thinking about it that way, a tablespoon-sized serving—plenty of pesto to dab on crostini or crudités—contains fewer than 60 calories. That's a perfect dose of deliciousness in my book!

2 cloves GARLIC

1 cup/115 g shelled unsalted roasted PISTACHIOS

24 large FRESH BASIL LEAVES, torn into small pieces

¼ cup/13 g coarsely chopped FRESH FLAT-LEAF PARSLEY

½ cup/60 g freshly grated PARMESAN CHEESE, preferably Parmigiano-Reggiano

¼ cup/60 ml EXTRA-VIRGIN OLIVE OIL

¼ cup/60 ml WATER

2 tbsp FRESH LEMON JUICE

½ tsp KOSHER OR SEA SALT

SKINNY DIPPERS: Bruschetta, Crostini, Baked Pita Chips, Crudités, Steamed Baby Artichokes, Poached Shrimp

In the workbowl of a food processor fitted with the metal blade, process the garlic until finely minced. Add the pistachios, basil, and parsley and pulse several times until finely chopped. Add the Parmesan and pulse just until combined. Add the olive oil, water, lemon juice, and salt. Process just until the pesto is well combined. Taste and adjust the seasoning. Transfer to a serving bowl and serve immediately.

DIP DO-AHEAD: The pesto can be prepared up to 3 days in advance. Cover and refrigerate. Remove from the refrigerator 45 minutes before serving. The pesto also freezes well: Place in a container with a tight-fitting lid and freeze for up to 2 months. Thaw in the refrigerator.

Artichoke Pesto

Here it is: an easy dip for artichoke lovers—fresh tasting, vibrant, with a lush undertone of garlic. With very little chopping and a quick pulse-pulse in a food processor, you have a terrific pesto that you can mound, dab, and scoop up to your heart's content.

2 cans (13.75 oz/390 g each) ARTICHOKE HEARTS packed in water, well drained

1/2 cup/60 g freshly grated PARMESAN CHEESE, preferably Parmigiano-Reggiano

1/4 cup/60 ml EXTRA-VIRGIN OLIVE OIL

2 tbsp FRESH LEMON JUICE

2 tbsp chopped FRESH FLAT-LEAF PARSLEY

1 tsp minced GARLIC

1 1/2 tsp KOSHER OR SEA SALT

1/4 tsp FRESHLY GROUND PEPPER

SKINNY DIPPERS: Bruschetta, Crostini, Baked Pita Chips

In the workbowl of a food processor fitted with the metal blade, process the artichokes until coarsely chopped. Add the Parmesan, olive oil, lemon juice, parsley, garlic, salt, and pepper and pulse several times until finely chopped. Taste and adjust the seasoning. Transfer to a serving bowl and serve immediately.

DIP DO-AHEAD: The pesto can be prepared up to 3 days in advance. Cover and refrigerate. Remove from the refrigerator 45 minutes before serving. Serve at room temperature.

MAKES

2 1/4

cups
(540 ml)

SERVING SIZE

2

tbsp

CALORIES	48
FAT	3.9 g
SAT	0.9 g
MONO	2.4 g
POLY	0.4 g
PROTEIN	2 g
CARB	2 g
FIBER	1 g
CHOL	2 mg
IRON	0.2 mg
SODIUM	194 mg
CALC	36 mg

SERVING SIZE

2

tbsp

CALORIES 48

FAT 3.1 g

SAT 0.5 g

MONO 1.1 g

POLY 1.3 g

PROTEIN 2 g

CARB 4 g

FIBER 1 g

CHOL 1 mg

IRON 0.3 mg

SODIUM 125 mg

CALC 47 mg

Turkish Zucchini & Walnut Dip

My husband, Greg, and I decided a few years ago to take our children, Eric and Molly, to Istanbul for a family vacation. We stayed in an apartment on the Asian side of the city, and most days we ferried across the Bosporus to visit the ancient sites, mosques, and palaces. We plotted our meals carefully so as to enjoy a broad tasting of Turkish cuisine. The kebabs, grilled fish (especially mackerel), braised dishes, breads, baklava, and appetizers were astonishing. This spread, one of the many I tasted in Istanbul, is a seductive, savory delight.

2 medium ZUCCHINI/COURGETTES (about 10 oz/280 g total)

1 tbsp EXTRA-VIRGIN OLIVE OIL

1 cup/240 ml LOW-FAT PLAIN YOGURT

½ cup/30 g crumbled fresh BREAD CRUMBS (from a baguette with the crust removed)

¼ cup/30 g finely chopped WALNUTS

1 tbsp minced GREEN/SPRING ONION

2½ tsp FRESH LEMON JUICE

1 tsp KOSHER OR SEA SALT

½ tsp minced GARLIC

¼ tsp FRESHLY GROUND PEPPER

Pinch or more of CAYENNE PEPPER

SKINNY DIPPERS: Baked Pita Chips, Crostini, Bruschetta, warmed wedges of fresh pita, lavash, cucumber slices

1. Using the fine grating surface on a box grater, grate the zucchini/courgettes. Place on a double thickness of paper towels/absorbent paper and squeeze out all the moisture. In a medium frying pan, preferably nonstick, warm the olive oil over medium heat. Add the zucchini/courgettes and sauté, stirring constantly, until all the moisture evaporates. Transfer to a cutting board and finely chop. Set aside until cool.

2. In a medium bowl, thoroughly mix together the yogurt, zucchini/courgettes, bread crumbs, walnuts, green/spring onion, lemon juice, salt, garlic, pepper, and cayenne. Taste and adjust the seasoning. (Adding as much as $\frac{1}{8}$ tsp of cayenne gives the dip a definite kick.) Transfer to a serving bowl. Serve immediately.

DIP DO-AHEAD: This dip can be prepared up to 1 day in advance. Cover and refrigerate. Remove from the refrigerator 20 minutes before serving.

CALORIES	32
FAT	2 g
SAT	1.2 g
MONO	0.6 g
POLY	0.1 g
PROTEIN	1 g
CARB	3 g
FIBER	0 g
CHOL	5 mg
IRON	0 mg
SODIUM	52 mg
CALC	22 mg

Horseradish Dunk

Every Passover, my maternal grandfather, Irving, made beet horse-radish from scratch. He was a gardener with a true green thumb when it came to tomatoes, but I can't remember if he grew his own horseradish. What I do remember is how teary-eyed everyone got when he served my grandmother's homemade gefilte fish with his beet horseradish on the side. Through the sniffles, we all expressed delight and assured him that this batch was the hottest and best yet. Horseradish is one of those flavors I have always loved. For all you other horseradish lovers out there, here's a fabulous dip. Use extra-hot prepared horseradish to guarantee those sniffles and teary eyes.

1 cup/240 ml REDUCED-FAT SOUR CREAM

¾ cup/105 g peeled, cored, and minced GRANNY SMITH APPLE

¼ cup/60 ml drained PREPARED HORSERADISH

2 tbsp minced WHITE ONION

2 tbsp FRESH LEMON JUICE

½ tsp KOSHER OR SEA SALT

¼ tsp FRESHLY GROUND PEPPER

¼ cup/12 g finely snipped FRESH CHIVES

SKINNY DIPPERS: Roasted Fingerling Potatoes, baked potato chips, wedges of tart apples, rolled slices of rare roast beef

In a medium bowl, whisk together the sour cream, apple, horse-radish, onion, lemon juice, salt, and pepper. Using a rubber spatula, fold in the chives. Refrigerate for at least 1 hour to allow the flavors to meld and the dip to thicken.

DIP DO-AHEAD: This dip can be prepared up to 1 day in advance. Cover and refrigerate. Remove from the refrigerator 10 minutes before serving.

Caramelized Sweet Onion Dip

We no longer need to think of onion dip as a package of dried onion-soup mix blended with sour cream and served with ridged potato chips. Instead, let's think about sweet onions slowly cooked in a hint of oil until they are soft, golden, and deeply, sweetly flavored. A creamy binding of sour cream and cream cheese speckled with freshly snipped chives turns this into an irresistible dip.

MAKES
about

2

cups
(480 ml)

SERVING SIZE

2

tbsp

CALORIES	60
FAT	3.9 g
SAT	2 g
MONO	1.5 g
POLY	0.2 g
PROTEIN	2 g
CARB	5 g
FIBER	0 g
CHOL	8 mg
IRON	0.2 mg
SODIUM	179 mg
CALC	40 mg

1 tbsp EXTRA-VIRGIN OLIVE OIL

2 medium WALLA WALLA OR OTHER SWEET ONIONS (about 1 lb/455 g), finely chopped

2 tsp KOSHER OR SEA SALT

1/4 tsp FRESHLY GROUND PEPPER

1 1/4 cups/300 ml REDUCED-FAT SOUR CREAM

2 oz/72 g LOW-FAT CREAM CHEESE (bar style), at room temperature

2 tsp WHITE WINE VINEGAR

1/4 cup/12 g finely snipped FRESH CHIVES

SKINNY DIPPERS: baked potato chips, Crostini, Baked Bagel Chips, Roasted Fingerling Potatoes, Crudités, thin breadsticks

1. In a large nonstick frying pan over medium-low heat, warm the olive oil and swirl to coat the pan. Add the onions, salt, and pepper. Sauté the onions, stirring frequently, until tender and caramelized to a golden hue (but not browned), 25 to 30 minutes. (Turn the heat to low, if necessary.) Remove from the heat and let cool to room temperature.

2. In a medium bowl, combine the sour cream, cream cheese, and vinegar. Using a rubber spatula, fold in the onions and then gently fold in the chives. Taste and adjust the seasoning.

DIP DO-AHEAD: This dip can be prepared up to 2 days in advance. Cover and refrigerate. Remove from the refrigerator 45 minutes before serving.

CALORIES	56
FAT	4.3 g
SAT	1.5 g
MONO	0.5 g
POLY	0.1 g
PROTEIN	2 g
CARB	2 g
FIBER	1 g
CHOL	8 mg
IRON	0.4 mg
SODIUM	194 mg
CALC	70 mg

Parmesan Spinach Dip

What makes this dip so different from the classic spinach dip recipes I've tasted is that it is made with reduced quantities of mayonnaise and sour cream—and low-fat versions of both, to boot. With no heavy binders to dull the flavor, the hint of fresh lemon zest, the under-current of garlic and onion, and the nutty flavor of the Parmesan all come through.

½ small WHITE ONION, roughly chopped

1 clove GARLIC, smashed

Grated zest of 1 large LEMON

1 tbsp FRESH LEMON JUICE

1 package (10 oz/280 g) FROZEN CHOPPED SPINACH, thawed and water squeezed out

½ cup/120 ml REDUCED-FAT MAYONNAISE

½ cup/120 ml REDUCED-FAT SOUR CREAM

½ cup/60 g freshly grated PARMESAN CHEESE, preferably Parmigiano-Reggiano

1 tsp KOSHER OR SEA SALT

½ tsp FRESHLY GROUND PEPPER

SKINNY DIPPERS: Crudités, Crostini, Baked Pita Chips, Baked Bagel Chips, baked potato chips, Seeded Tortilla Chips

In the workbowl of a food processor fitted with the metal blade, process the onion, garlic, and lemon zest until finely minced. Add the spinach and pulse several times until finely chopped. Add the mayonnaise, sour cream, Parmesan, lemon juice, salt, and pepper. Process just until the dip is well mixed but not puréed smooth. Taste and adjust the seasoning. Transfer to a serving bowl and serve immediately.

DIP DO-AHEAD: This dip can be prepared up to 1 day in advance. Cover and refrigerate. Remove from the refrigerator 20 minutes before serving.

MAKES

about

1 1/2

cups
(360 ml)

SERVING SIZE

2

tbsp

CALORIES 28
....
FAT 2.3 g
SAT 0.3 g
MONO 1.7 g
POLY 0.3 g
....
PROTEIN 0 g
CARB 2 g
FIBER 0 g
CHOL 0 mg
IRON 0.4 mg
SODIUM 102 mg
CALC 7 mg

Roasted Tomato Spread

Roasting tomatoes intensifies their flavor and concentrates the juices, making even out-of-season plum tomatoes taste good. I love the bright, robust flavors of this spread, as well as its appearance— burnished red with specks of green. This spread is perfect on bruschetta, crostini, and grilled eggplant.

2 lb/910 g PLUM TOMATOES, cored, halved, and seeded

1/2 tsp KOSHER OR SEA SALT

1/2 tsp SUGAR

1 tbsp BALSAMIC VINEGAR

2 tbsp ROASTED-GARLIC OLIVE OIL

1/2 cup/25 g minced FRESH FLAT-LEAF PARSLEY

FRESHLY GROUND PEPPER

SKINNY DIPPERS: Bruschetta, Crostini, Parmesan-Crusted Pita Chips, Grilled Japanese Eggplant

1. Preheat the oven to 350°F/180°C/gas 4. In a large bowl, toss the tomato halves with the salt, sugar, vinegar, and 1 tbsp of the oil until thoroughly coated. Arrange cut-side up in a 9-by-13-in/ 20-by-30-cm baking dish. Use a rubber spatula to scrape any remaining juices from the bowl over the tomatoes. Cover the dish with aluminum foil and roast the tomatoes in the oven for 30 min-utes. Uncover and roast the tomatoes until they are completely softened, 30 minutes longer. Set aside to cool for 10 minutes.

2. Put the tomatoes and all the juices from the pan in the workbowl of a food processor fitted with the metal blade. Process until puréed and smooth. Add the remaining 1 tbsp of oil, the parsley, and a few grinds of pepper. Pulse several times to combine. Taste and adjust the seasoning. Transfer to a serving bowl, cover, and set aside at room temperature until ready to serve, up to 2 hours.

DIP DO-AHEAD: This spread can be prepared up to 5 days in advance. Cover and refrigerate. Serve at room temperature.

Roasted Red Pepper Spread with Basil & Capers

CALORIES	71
FAT	6.6 g
SAT	0.9 g
MONO	2.7 g
POLY	2 g
PROTEIN	1 g
CARB	3 g
FIBER	1 g
CHOL	1 mg
IRON	0.4 mg
SODIUM	190 mg
CALC	11 mg

If you are in a hurry, or just don't want to bother roasting your own peppers, use store-bought roasted peppers that come in a jar. Blot them dry with paper towels/absorbent paper, dice them, and they're ready to use.

2 large RED BELL PEPPERS/CAPSICUMS, roasted (see page 16) and finely diced

12 oil-packed SUN-DRIED TOMATOES, drained (reserving 4 tsp of the oil), and very finely diced

12 large FRESH BASIL LEAVES, minced

4 oil-packed ANCHOVY FILLETS, rinsed, blotted dry, and minced

2 tbsp CAPERS, rinsed and blotted dry

2 tsp finely minced GARLIC

2 tsp FRESH LEMON JUICE

1/2 tsp FRESHLY GROUND PEPPER

1/4 tsp KOSHER OR SEA SALT

SKINNY DIPPERS: Bruschetta, Crostini, Baked Pita Chips, Baked Bagel Chips, warm pita bread

In a medium bowl, combine the roasted peppers/capsicums, tomatoes, basil, anchovies, capers, and garlic. Stir in the lemon juice and reserved sun-dried tomato oil, then add the pepper and salt. Taste and adjust the seasoning. Transfer to a serving bowl, cover, and set aside at room temperature until ready to serve, up to 3 hours.

DIP DO-AHEAD: This dip can be prepared up to 3 days in advance. Cover and refrigerate. Remove from the refrigerator 45 minutes before serving. Serve at room temperature.

 CHAPTER 2

Salsas, Guacamoles, and Tapenades

When it comes to dipping and indulging, salsas are a dieter's delight, since their flavor factor is pumped up and their caloric content turned down. Eat a lip-buzzing half cup/120 ml of Skinny Tomato Salsa and you've only ingested 22 calories and less than a gram of fat. Turn peak-season peaches into Minted Peach Salsa and set the mood for a sizzling summer party with big flavor and miraculously few calories. Even avocados, considered one of the most nutrient-dense foods, can be eaten in moderation, especially when mingled with mangoes in the luscious Mango Guacamole.

CALORIES   11
....
FAT   0.1 g
SAT   0 g
MONO   0 g
POLY   0 g
....
PROTEIN   0 g
CARB   3 g
FIBER   1 g
CHOL   0 mg
IRON   0.2 mg
SODIUM   51 mg
CALC   9 mg

Skinny Tomato Salsa

Of course it is easy to pick up a container of store-bought salsa for entertaining, but the tomato flavor is never as vibrant nor the herbs as fresh tasting as with homemade salsa. When tomato season is in full force, I make a big batch of tomato salsa. Buy whatever tomatoes look best at the market—think about using heirloom varieties such as Brandywine, Green Zebra, or Big Rainbow.

4 large PLUM TOMATOES, cored, seeded, and cut into
  1/2-in/12-mm dice (about 1 3/4 cups/337 g)

1 JALAPEÑO CHILE, seeds and ribs removed, minced (see page 16)

2 GREEN/SPRING ONIONS, including green tops, cut crosswise into
  thin slices

3/4 cup/100 g diced RED ONION

1/2 cup/ 30 g chopped CILANTRO/FRESH CORIANDER LEAVES

1/2 tsp minced GARLIC

1 1/2 tbsp FRESH LEMON JUICE

1 1/2 tbsp FRESH LIME JUICE

1 tsp SUGAR

1/2 tsp GROUND CORIANDER

1/2 tsp GROUND CUMIN

1/4 tsp KOSHER OR SEA SALT
....

SKINNY DIPPERS: Baked Tortilla Chips, Baked Pita Chips

In a medium bowl, combine the tomatoes, jalapeño, green/spring onions, red onion, cilantro/fresh coriander, and garlic. In a measuring cup, stir together the lemon juice, lime juice, sugar, ground coriander, cumin, and salt. Stir until the sugar and salt dissolve and then pour over the tomato mixture. Stir gently to combine. Transfer to a serving bowl, cover, and set aside for at least 1 hour to allow the flavors to meld.

DIP DO-AHEAD: This salsa is best when made within 6 hours of serving, but it can be prepared up to 1 day in advance. Cover and refrigerate. Remove from the refrigerator 45 minutes before serving.

Salsa Italiana— Cherry Tomatoes, Roasted Garlic, and Basil

Let's commingle cultural traditions by turning classic Mexican salsa ingredients—tomatoes, peppers, and onions—into an Italian affair with the addition of roasted garlic, fresh basil, and oregano. If you plan ahead and have a head of roasted garlic ready to use, this salsa is a cinch to make on the day of the party. Roasted garlic is a boon to the calorie-conscious cook because it adds big flavor but few calories. As you'll see, only a minuscule amount of olive oil is used in this recipe. I love to serve this salsa as a dip, but I also adore it as an accompaniment to grilled halibut skewers or pan-seared red snapper.

1 head GARLIC

2 cups/350 g CHERRY TOMATOES, stemmed and quartered

1 YELLOW BELL PEPPER/CAPSICUM, seeded, deribbed, and cut into ½-in/12-mm dice (about 1 cup/152 g)

½ cup/70 g diced RED ONION

¼ cup/15 g chopped FRESH BASIL LEAVES

2 tbsp chopped FRESH OREGANO LEAVES

2 tbsp FRESH LEMON JUICE

1 tbsp RED WINE VINEGAR

1 tsp KOSHER OR SEA SALT

½ tsp CRUSHED RED PEPPER

1 tsp EXTRA-VIRGIN OLIVE OIL

....

SKINNY DIPPERS: Bruschetta, Crostini, Poached Shrimp

1. Preheat the oven to 375°F/190°C/gas 5. Roast the head of garlic as directed on page 17. (While the garlic is roasting, chop the vegetables and herbs.)

CONTINUED »

SERVING SIZE

1/4

cup
(60 ml)

CALORIES	20
FAT	0.5 g
SAT	0.1 g
MONO	0.3 g
POLY	0.1 g
PROTEIN	1 g
CARB	4 g
FIBER	1 g
CHOL	0 mg
IRON	0.3 mg
SODIUM	99 mg
CALC	15.6 mg

2. In a medium bowl, whisk together the lemon juice, vinegar, salt, and crushed red pepper until the salt is dissolved. Remove the warm cloves of garlic from their skins and add to the vinegar mixture. Using a fork, mash the roasted garlic until puréed smooth. Whisk in the olive oil.

3. Add the tomatoes, bell pepper/capsicum, and onion and gently mix to coat with the dressing. Fold in the basil and oregano. Taste and adjust the seasoning. Transfer to a serving bowl, cover, and set aside for at least 1 hour to allow the flavors to meld.

DIP DO-AHEAD: This salsa can be prepared up to 8 hours in advance. Cover and refrigerate. Remove from the refrigerator 45 minutes before serving.

Fiery Black Bean, Roasted Corn, and Jicama Salsa

This recipe calls for you to grill the corn, as it brings out the natural sugars and adds a wonderful caramelized flavor to the salsa. If that step seems too time-consuming, or you aren't planning to fire up a grill for the rest of your meal, here is a simpler alternative: Remove the corn from the cob with a knife and pan-roast the kernels in a heavy-bottomed frying pan, preferably cast iron, over medium heat with two teaspoons of olive oil until they are caramel brown. Be sure to stir frequently so the corn doesn't blacken. Another option is to use an indoor grill pan and grill the corn as directed for outdoor grilling.

1 large ear FRESH CORN, husk on

2 tsp EXTRA-VIRGIN OLIVE OIL

1¼ tsp KOSHER OR SEA SALT

FRESHLY GROUND PEPPER

Juice of 2 LIMES

1 tsp GROUND CUMIN

1 tsp GROUND CORIANDER

2 tsp packed BROWN SUGAR

1 can (15 oz/430 g) BLACK BEANS, drained and rinsed

¾ cup/110 g peeled and diced JICAMA

¼ cup/35 g diced RED ONION

1 SERRANO CHILE, including seeds and ribs, finely minced (see page 16)

2 GREEN/SPRING ONIONS, including green tops, cut on the diagonal into thin slices

⅓ cup/20 g chopped CILANTRO/FRESH CORIANDER LEAVES

SKINNY DIPPERS: Baked Tortilla Chips, Baked Pita Chips, Poached Shrimp

1. Prepare a medium-hot fire in a charcoal grill/barbecue, preheat a gas grill/barbecue on medium-high, or place a stovetop ridged grill pan over medium-high heat.

2. Pull back the husk from the corn without actually removing it. Remove the silk and brush the corn with 1 tsp of the oil. Sprinkle the corn lightly with ¼ tsp of the salt and a little pepper. Pull up the husk to cover the corn and twist at the top to enclose the corn.

3. When the grill is hot, arrange the corn on the grill grate directly over the fire. Cover the grill and cook the corn on one side, for about 5 minutes. Turn the corn and cover the grill again. Give the corn one more turn and continue grilling just until the corn begins picking up color without blackening, about 2 minutes longer. Remove the corn from the grill and let cool.

4. Meanwhile, in a medium bowl, whisk together the lime juice, cumin, ground coriander, brown sugar, and the remaining 1 tsp of salt until dissolved. Whisk in the remaining 1 tsp of olive oil.

5. Stand the ear of corn upright, stem-side down, on a cutting board. Using a sharp knife, cut downward along the cob, removing the kernels and rotating the corn a quarter turn after each cut. Discard the cob and scoop the kernels into the bowl with the dressing. Add the beans, jicama, red onion, and serrano chile. Gently mix to coat with the dressing. Fold in the green/spring onions and cilantro/fresh coriander. Taste and adjust the seasoning. Transfer to a serving bowl, cover, and set aside for at least 1 hour to allow the flavors to meld.

DIP DO-AHEAD: This salsa can be prepared up to 2 days in advance. Cover and refrigerate. Remove from the refrigerator 45 minutes before serving.

Green Mango Salsa

This dip is big, bright, and boldly spiced—a vibrantly hued salsa that is deliriously delicious, punctuated with cilantro/fresh coriander, and power-surged with jalapeño chile. If you and your friends love the heat, use two whole chiles; one is plenty for me.

1 very large, green (unripe) MANGO, peeled, pitted, and cut into ½-in/12-mm dice

¾ cup/115 g diced RED BELL PEPPER/CAPSICUM

½ cup/70 g diced RED ONION

1 large JALAPEÑO CHILE, including seeds and ribs, minced (see page 16)

¼ cup/15 g chopped CILANTRO/FRESH CORIANDER LEAVES

2 tbsp FRESH LIME JUICE

1 tsp KOSHER OR SEA SALT

⅛ tsp FRESHLY GROUND PEPPER

SKINNY DIPPERS: Baked Tortilla Chips, Baked Wonton Crisps, Poached Shrimp

In a large bowl, combine the mango, bell pepper/capsicum, onion, jalapeño, cilantro/fresh coriander, and lime juice. Add the salt and pepper and stir to combine. Transfer to a serving bowl, cover, and set aside for at least 1 hour to allow the flavors to meld.

DIP DO-AHEAD: This salsa can be prepared up to 2 days in advance. Cover and refrigerate. Remove from the refrigerator 45 minutes before serving.

MAKES about

3½

cups
(840 ml)

SERVING SIZE

¼

cup
(60 ml)

CALORIES	20
FAT	0.1 g
SAT	0 g
MONO	0 g
POLY	0 g
PROTEIN	0 g
CARB	5 g
FIBER	1 g
CHOL	0 mg
IRON	0.1 mg
SODIUM	84 mg
CALC	5 mg

CALORIES	46
FAT	1.6 g
SAT	0.2 g
MONO	0.9 g
POLY	0.2 g
PROTEIN	1 g
CARB	8 g
FIBER	2 g
CHOL	0 mg
IRON	0.2 mg
SODIUM	75 mg
CALC	18 mg

Pomegranate, Orange, and Avocado Salsa

Creating a dip with the properly creamy mouthfeel while reducing the calories and fat means kicking up the flavor with wintry fruits. Chunks of navel orange add a tropical zest, while the pomegranate seeds add sparkling color and an appealing crunch. If you want to make this salsa zippier, add the seeds and ribs from the jalapeño or substitute a serrano or two, which are even spicier. While this salsa is fabulous with chips, also think about using it to accompany seared salmon or scallops, grilled shrimp/prawn skewers, or just about any preparation of fish.

1 tbsp FRESH LIME JUICE

1 tsp KOSHER OR SEA SALT

1/8 tsp FRESHLY GROUND PEPPER

3 large NAVEL ORANGES

1 POMEGRANATE

1 large HASS AVOCADO, halved, pitted, peeled, and cut into 1/2-in/12-mm dice

2/3 cup/90 g diced RED ONION

1 JALAPEÑO CHILE, seeds and ribs removed, minced (see page 16)

2 GREEN/SPRING ONIONS, including green tops, cut on the diagonal into thin slices

1/4 cup/15 g chopped CILANTRO/FRESH CORIANDER LEAVES

SKINNY DIPPERS: Baked Tortilla Chips, Baked Wonton Crisps, Poached Shrimp

1. In a large bowl, whisk together the lime juice, salt, and pepper until the salt dissolves.

2. Working with one orange at a time, cut a slice from the top and bottom to reveal the flesh. Stand the orange upright and slice away the peel from the sides in wide strips, cutting downward, following the contour of the fruit, and removing all the white pith. Holding the orange over a bowl, use a sharp paring knife to

cut along both sides of each segment, releasing the segments and allowing the juice and segments to drop into the bowl. Discard any seeds that might adhere to the fruit or drop into the bowl. Repeat with the remaining oranges. (This technique is called "supreming.") Drain the juice into a measuring cup and set aside. Cut the orange segments into ½-in/12-mm pieces and add to the bowl containing the lime juice.

3. To extract the seeds from the pomegranate, cut the fruit into quarters. Fill a large bowl with cold water and place it in the kitchen sink to contain any squirting pomegranate juice. Using your fingertips, break the seeds away from the pith under water. (I wear disposable surgical gloves that I buy at the pharmacy to keep my fingers from being stained red.) The seeds will sink to the bottom of the bowl. Discard any pith, drain the water, blot the seeds lightly with paper towels/absorbent paper, and add to the bowl with the orange segments.

4. Add the avocado, red onion, jalapeño, green/spring onions, and cilantro/fresh coriander to the bowl. Using a rubber spatula, gently fold the ingredients together, being careful to not mash the avocado. Add the reserved orange juice, 1 tbsp at a time, until the salsa is moist but not soupy. Taste and adjust the seasoning. Transfer to a serving bowl, cover, and set aside for at least 1 hour to allow the flavors to meld.

DIP DO-AHEAD: This salsa can be prepared up to 8 hours in advance. (If prepared too far ahead of time, the avocados will begin to discolor.) Cover and refrigerate. Remove from the refrigerator 45 minutes before serving.

CALORIES	61
FAT	0.2 g
SAT	0 g
MONO	0 g
POLY	0 g
PROTEIN	1 g
CARB	16 g
FIBER	0 g
CHOL	0 mg
IRON	0.4 mg
SODIUM	67 mg
CALC	20 mg

Pineapple, Red Pepper, and Jalapeño Salsa

This colorful, fiery salsa is a great partner for baked chips. However, it is also a great complement for grilled pork tenderloin, ham/gammon steaks, grilled tuna, salmon, and snapper. One jalapeño chile, with the seeds and ribs included, makes the salsa plenty hot, but add more if you like.

2 tbsp FRESH LIME JUICE

1 tbsp packed LIGHT BROWN SUGAR

¹/₂ tsp KOSHER OR SEA SALT

¹/₂ PINEAPPLE, peeled, halved lengthwise, cored, and cut into ¹/₄-in/6-mm dice

1 small RED BELL PEPPER/CAPSICUM, seeded, deribbed, and cut into ¹/₄-in/6-mm dice

2 GREEN/SPRING ONIONS, including green tops, halved lengthwise and thinly sliced

1 JALAPEÑO CHILE, including seeds and ribs, minced (see page 16)

1 tsp chopped FRESH THYME LEAVES

SKINNY DIPPERS: Baked Tortilla Chips, Baked Wonton Crisps, Poached Shrimp

1. In a large bowl, whisk together the lime juice, brown sugar, and salt until the salt dissolves.

2. Add the pineapple, bell pepper/capsicum, green/spring onions, jalapeño, and thyme, and gently mix to coat with the dressing. Taste and adjust the seasoning. Transfer to a serving bowl, cover, and set aside for at least 1 hour to allow the flavors to meld.

DIP DO-AHEAD: This salsa can be prepared up to 2 days in advance. Cover and refrigerate. Remove from the refrigerator 45 minutes before serving.

Minted Peach Salsa

Picture a summer evening patio party with a group of friends, glasses of prosecco or a great microbrew in hand, and a platter of skewers ready to barbecue. Start with a bowl of this minted peach salsa and some baked chips or cold poached shrimp/prawns. Follow the chips and dip with a mixed-grill dinner of seafood skewers, marinated pork or chicken, and summer vegetables—a casual and completely relaxed way to entertain.

Grated zest of 1 LIME

1 to 2 tbsp FRESH LIME JUICE

1 tsp KOSHER OR SEA SALT

1/8 tsp FRESHLY GROUND PEPPER

3 large, firm but ripe FREESTONE PEACHES, peeled and cut into 1/2-in/12-mm dice

1/2 cup/70 g diced RED ONION

1 JALAPEÑO CHILE, seeds and ribs removed, minced (see page 16)

1/4 cup/15 g chopped FRESH MINT

....

SKINNY DIPPERS: Baked Tortilla Chips, Baked Wonton Crisps, Poached Shrimp

In a medium bowl, whisk together the lime zest and juice, salt, and pepper until the salt is dissolved. Add the peaches, onion, jalapeño, and mint. Mix gently to combine. Taste and adjust the seasoning. Transfer to a serving bowl, cover, and set aside for at least 1 hour to allow the flavors to meld.

DIP DO-AHEAD: This salsa can be prepared up to 8 hours in advance. Cover and refrigerate. Remove from the refrigerator 45 minutes before serving.

MAKES about

3

cups
(720 ml)

SERVING SIZE

1/4

cup
(60 ml)

CALORIES	22
FAT	0.1 g
SAT	0 g
MONO	0 g
POLY	0 g
PROTEIN	1 g
CARB	6 g
FIBER	1 g
CHOL	0 mg
IRON	0.4 mg
SODIUM	98 mg
CALC	9 mg

SERVING SIZE

1/4

cup
(60 ml)

CALORIES	53
FAT	4.4 g
SAT	0.6 g
MONO	2.8 g
POLY	0.6 g
PROTEIN	1 g
CARB	4 g
FIBER	2 g
CHOL	0 mg
IRON	0.3 mg
SODIUM	52 mg
CALC	7 mg

Tomatillo Guacamole

Tomatillos, also called Mexican green tomatoes, belong to the night-shade family. They resemble small green tomatoes except that the tomatillos have a papery husk. Look for firm fruit with dry, intact husks.

4 TOMATILLOS, papery husks removed, halved lengthwise

2 large PLUM TOMATOES, cored, halved lengthwise, and seeded

2 tsp CANOLA OIL

2 large HASS AVOCADOS, halved, pitted, and peeled

1/2 cup/30 g chopped CILANTRO/FRESH CORIANDER LEAVES

1/4 cup/35 g diced RED ONION

3 SERRANO CHILES, seeds and ribs removed, minced (see page 16)

2 tbsp FRESH LIME JUICE

1/2 tsp KOSHER OR SEA SALT

SKINNY DIPPERS: Baked Tortilla Chips, Crudités, Poached Shrimp

1. Prepare a medium-hot fire in a charcoal grill/barbecue, pre-heat a gas grill/barbecue on medium-high, or place a stovetop ridged grill pan over medium-high heat.

2. Brush the tomatillos and tomatoes with the oil. Place the tomatillos and tomatoes, cut-side down, directly over the fire. Cover the grill and cook, turning once, until dark brown grill marks appear and they are tender, about 3 minutes per side. Transfer to a cutting board and cut into 1/2-in/12-mm dice. Set aside.

3. In a medium bowl, mash the avocados until chunky. Add the grilled tomatillos and tomatoes. Fold in the cilantro/fresh cori-ander, onion, serrano chiles, lime juice, and salt. Transfer to a serving bowl and serve immediately.

DIP DO-AHEAD: This dip is best when made within 8 hours of serv-ing, but it can be prepared up to 1 day in advance. Place a piece of plastic wrap/cling film directly on the surface of the guacamole. Remove from the refrigerator 30 minutes before serving, but keep covered until ready to serve.

SERVING SIZE

¼

cup
(60 ml)

CALORIES	36
FAT	1.6 g
SAT	0.2 g
MONO	1 g
POLY	0.2 g
PROTEIN	0 g
CARB	6 g
FIBER	1 g
CHOL	0 mg
IRON	0.2 mg
SODIUM	127 mg
CALC	8 mg

Mango Guacamole

As anyone who has cut into an avocado knows, the flesh begins to turn brown when exposed to air. That is true for guacamole, too, though the addition of lemon or lime juice can help to slow discoloration. What makes this guacamole so terrific—besides its lively, luscious taste and low calorie count—is that the mango prevents the guacamole from discoloring altogether. Honestly, I was amazed when I developed this recipe. Even after two days in the refrigerator, the guacamole remained beautifully green and fresh tasting.

1 large, ripe MANGO, peeled, pitted, and coarsely chopped

1 large, ripe HASS AVOCADO, halved, pitted, peeled, and coarsely chopped

¾ cup/100 g roughly chopped RED ONION

3 tbsp seeded and minced JALAPEÑO CHILE (see page 16)

½ tsp minced GARLIC

⅓ cup/35 g thinly sliced GREEN/SPRING ONIONS, including green tops

½ tbsp FRESH LIME JUICE

1½ tsp KOSHER OR SEA SALT

SKINNY DIPPERS: Baked Tortilla Chips, Baked Wonton Crisps, Poached Shrimp

In the workbowl of a food processor fitted with the metal blade, pulse the mango, avocado, red onion, jalapeño, and garlic until creamy and finely textured but not puréed. Transfer to a bowl and stir in the green/spring onions, lime juice, and salt. Taste and adjust the seasoning. Transfer to a serving bowl and serve immediately.

DIP DO-AHEAD: This dip can be prepared up to 2 days in advance. Cover and refrigerate. (It's not critical to press a piece of plastic wrap/cling film directly on the surface of the guacamole to prevent discoloration, but it helps to keep it fresh.) Remove from the refrigerator 30 minutes before serving.

Creamy Avocado Dip

A one-dip wonder—luscious and dreamy, with a designer pale buttery-green hue. How can this recipe be in a book on skinny dips? Indeed, avocados have an exceptionally high fat content, accounting for more than 75 percent of the calories in the fruit. However, the fat in avocados is the "good and healthful" monounsaturated variety, which does not raise blood cholesterol, and avocados are one of the top ten nutrient-dense foods. Serve an abundance of fresh, crisp veggies alongside the dip and scoop in moderation.

2 large, ripe HASS AVOCADOS, halved, pitted, peeled, and coarsely chopped

½ cup/120 ml REDUCED-FAT SOUR CREAM

2 tbsp finely minced SHALLOTS

1½ tbsp seeded and minced JALAPEÑO CHILE (see page 16)

1½ tbsp FRESH LIME JUICE

½ tsp minced GARLIC

1 tsp KOSHER OR SEA SALT

....

SKINNY DIPPERS: Crudités, Baked Tortilla Chips, baked potato chips

In the workbowl of a food processor fitted with the metal blade, process the avocados, sour cream, shallots, jalapeño, lime juice, garlic, and salt until smooth, scraping down the sides of the bowl as necessary. Taste and adjust the seasoning. Transfer to a serving bowl and serve immediately.

DIP DO-AHEAD: This dip is best when made within 8 hours of serving, but it can be prepared up to 1 day in advance. Place a piece of plastic wrap/cling film directly on the surface of the dip, pressing to eliminate any air pockets before refrigerating. (This will help keep the dip from turning brown.) Remove from the refrigerator 30 minutes before serving, but keep covered until ready to serve.

MAKES about

2½

cups (600 ml)

SERVING SIZE

2

tbsp

CALORIES	34
FAT	2.9 g
SAT	0.8 g
MONO	1.6 g
POLY	0.3 g
PROTEIN	1 g
CARB	2 g
FIBER	1 g
CHOL	2 mg
IRON	0.1 mg
SODIUM	63 mg
CALC	10 mg

SERVING SIZE

1/4

cup
(60 ml)

CALORIES	55
FAT	4.7 g
SAT	0.6 g
MONO	3.4 g
POLY	0.5 g
PROTEIN	1 g
CARB	3 g
FIBER	1 g
CHOL	0 mg
IRON	0.5 mg
SODIUM	261 mg
CALC	17 mg

Smoky Red Pepper, Sweet Onion, and Olive Tapenade

This versatile, Mediterranean-inspired olive tapenade is perfect for summer entertaining, especially when you are planning a grilled meal. Top bruschetta or crostini with this tapenade for an appetizer, but don't stop there. I have served a generous spoonful or two as an accompaniment to grilled chicken, pork tenderloin, bone-in pork chops, or grilled leg of lamb. Sliced flank steak, hot off the grill, is a sensation when paired with this smoky olive tapenade. And it pairs well with grilled fish such as halibut, swordfish, tuna, and salmon. I intentionally developed this recipe to make a large quantity, because in addition to all the uses noted above, it is terrific when tossed into pasta for either a hot main dish or a cold summer salad.

2 large RED BELL PEPPERS/CAPSICUMS, quartered, seeded, and deribbed

1 medium WALLA WALLA OR OTHER SWEET ONION, cut crosswise into 1/2-in/12-mm thick slices

4 tbsp/60 ml EXTRA-VIRGIN OLIVE OIL

2/3 cup/85 g pitted GREEN OLIVES, sliced into rounds

2/3 cup/140 g pitted RIPE BLACK OLIVES, sliced into rounds

1/4 cup/40 g CAPERS, rinsed and blotted dry

1/4 cup/13 g minced FRESH FLAT-LEAF PARSLEY

1 large clove GARLIC, minced

1 tbsp BALSAMIC VINEGAR

1/2 tsp KOSHER OR SEA SALT

1/2 tsp FRESHLY GROUND PEPPER

SKINNY DIPPERS: Bruschetta, Crostini, Poached Shrimp, Baked Pita Chips, lavash

1. Prepare a medium-hot fire in a charcoal grill/barbecue, pre-heat a gas grill/barbecue on medium-high, or place a stovetop ridged grill pan over medium-high heat.

2. Brush the bell peppers/capsicums and onion slices with 1½ tbsp of the olive oil. Place the vegetables directly over the fire. Cover the grill and cook, turning once, until dark brown grill marks appear and the vegetables are crisp-tender, 4 to 5 minutes. Transfer to a cutting board.

3. Cut the grilled vegetables into ½-in/12-mm dice. Transfer to a large bowl. Add the green and black olives, capers, parsley, and garlic. Add the remaining 2½ tbsp olive oil and the vinegar, salt, and pepper. Using a rubber spatula, gently stir the tapenade to combine. Transfer to a serving bowl and serve immediately.

DIP DO-AHEAD: This tapenade can be prepared up to 3 days in advance. Cover and refrigerate. Remove from the refrigerator 45 minutes before serving.

CALORIES	47
FAT	4.4 g
SAT	0.5 g
MONO	3.1 g
POLY	0.7 g
PROTEIN	1 g
CARB	2 g
FIBER	1 g
CHOL	0 mg
IRON	0.3 mg
SODIUM	276 mg
CALC	21 mg

Green Olive and Almond Tapenade

Using ripe green olives, celery, smoked almonds, and no olive oil, I improvise on the classic Provençal olive spread in order to cut calories yet kick up the flavor. Trust me, it's addictively delicious. For an appetizer, slather the tapenade on toasted or grilled bread or serve it in a bowl and let your guests spoon it on themselves. The tapenade could even be used as a condiment for grilled vegetables or fish. Add a touch of reduced-fat mayonnaise and blend it with hard-cooked egg yolks for indulgent yet light deviled eggs.

¼ cup/30 g smoked salted ALMONDS

1 can (6 oz/170 g, drained weight) pitted RIPE GREEN OLIVES, drained

¼ cup/35 g thinly sliced CELERY

1 tbsp chopped FRESH FLAT-LEAF PARSLEY

1 clove GARLIC, roughly chopped

1 tsp minced FRESH THYME LEAVES

Grated zest of ½ LEMON

1 tbsp FRESH LEMON JUICE

1 tbsp RED WINE VINEGAR

¼ tsp FRESHLY GROUND PEPPER

SKINNY DIPPERS: Crostini, Bruschetta, Baked Pita Chips, Steamed Baby Artichokes, Belgian endive/chicory, lavash

In the workbowl of a food processor fitted with the metal blade, process the almonds until finely chopped. Add the olives, celery, parsley, garlic, thyme, lemon zest and juice, vinegar, and pepper. Pulse until uniformly minced, scraping down the sides of the bowl once or twice. Transfer to a serving bowl, cover, and set aside for at least 1 hour to allow the flavors to meld.

DIP DO-AHEAD: This tapenade can be prepared up to 3 days in advance. Cover and refrigerate. Remove from the refrigerator 45 minutes before serving.

Cheese and Tofu Dips

Take a global, palate-pleasing excursion through this chapter, which is filled with protein-rich, vegetarian-friendly dips and spreads made with cheese and tofu. Dunk into the Asian flavors of the delicately seasoned Edamame Tofu Dip, a nutrient wonder. Head to Greece for the sunny and seductive tastes of Baked Feta Spinach Dip—a bubbly party starter and waistline keeper. Go all-American at your next Super Bowl party with the skinny Chorizo Chile Con Queso Lite and skip the goopy orange stuff served at the ballpark. These real-deal dips are punctuated with taste and styled for slimness.

3
cups
(720 ml)

SERVING SIZE

2
tbsp

CALORIES	34
FAT	2.2 g
SAT	0.3 g
MONO	0.7 g
POLY	1 g
PROTEIN	2 g
CARB	2 g
FIBER	1 g
CHOL	0 mg
IRON	0.4 mg
SODIUM	99 mg
CALC	21 mg

Edamame Tofu Dip

I almost always have a bag of frozen shelled edamame in my freezer. Here I purée them for a creamy, fresh, protein-packed dip speckled with cilantro.

1 cup/225 g SILKEN TOFU

2 cups/290 g frozen shelled EDAMAME

2 tsp KOSHER OR SEA SALT

3 tbsp FRESH LEMON JUICE

2 tbsp ASIAN SESAME OIL

1 tsp finely minced GARLIC

1 tsp SUGAR

1 tsp FRESHLY GROUND PEPPER

1/4 cup/15 g minced CILANTRO/FRESH CORIANDER LEAVES, plus sprigs for garnish

SKINNY DIPPERS: Baked Pita Chips, Crudités, Crostini

1. Drain the tofu and blot completely dry with paper towels/absorbent paper. Set the tofu on several thicknesses of paper while you cook the edamame.

2. Fill a medium saucepan two-thirds full of water and bring to a boil over high heat. Add the edamame and 1/2 tsp of the salt and boil for 3 minutes. Drain in a colander and rinse under cold water. Drain again and blot to remove excess moisture.

3. In the workbowl of a food processor fitted with the metal blade, process the tofu, edamame, the remaining 1 1/2 tsp salt, the lemon juice, sesame oil, garlic, sugar, and pepper until very smooth. Scatter the minced cilantro/fresh coriander leaves over the top and pulse to incorporate. Taste and adjust the seasoning. Transfer to a serving bowl, cover, and refrigerate for at least 1 hour to allow the flavors to meld. Garnish with cilantro/fresh coriander.

DIP DO-AHEAD: This dip can be prepared up to 2 days in advance. Cover and refrigerate. Remove from the refrigerator just before serving.

SERVING SIZE

2

tbsp

CALORIES	65
FAT	6.1 g
SAT	0.9 g
MONO	1.7 g
POLY	3.3 g
PROTEIN	2 g
CARB	1 g
FIBER	0 g
CHOL	0 mg
IRON	0.5 mg
SODIUM	121 mg
CALC	50 mg

Curried Tofu Pâté

As tempting as it might be to make this pâté using a food processor, I much prefer its texture when the tofu is mashed with a fork. Serve the pâté as a dip, of course, but also consider it as a lunchtime option.

1 lb/455 g FIRM TOFU

2 tsp CANOLA OIL

3 GREEN/SPRING ONIONS, including green tops, finely diced

1 rib CELERY, finely diced

2 tsp CURRY POWDER

Pinch or two of CAYENNE PEPPER

½ cup/120 ml REDUCED-FAT MAYONNAISE

¼ cup/25 g minced FRESH FLAT-LEAF PARSLEY

2 tsp HONEY

1½ tsp KOSHER OR SEA SALT

¼ tsp FRESHLY GROUND PEPPER

SKINNY DIPPERS: Crostini, Baked Pita Chips, Baked Bagel Chips, Crudités, Bruschetta, Marbled Rye Toasts

1. Drain the tofu and blot completely dry with paper towels/absorbent paper. In a small nonstick frying pan over medium heat, warm the oil. Add the green/spring onions and celery and sauté to soften, about 1 minute. Add the curry powder and cayenne. Sauté until the spices are fragrant, about 1 minute longer. Remove from the heat.

2. In a medium bowl, mash the tofu with a fork. Stir in the curry mixture. Add the mayonnaise, parsley, honey, salt, and pepper. Gently mix to combine. Transfer to a serving bowl and serve immediately.

DIP DO-AHEAD: This dip can be prepared up to 3 days in advance. Cover and refrigerate. Serve chilled but not refrigerator cold.

Baked Feta Spinach Dip

When you peel away the flaky layers of buttered phyllo from the classic Greek pie called *spanakopita*, you have a delectably savory filling of sautéed spinach and onions mixed with feta cheese, eggs, and seasonings. I've taken some liberties here and created this Greek-style baked spinach dip with sweet onions, garlic, and lemon zest. However, I've reduced the fat and lightened up on the calories.

1 package (16 oz/455 g) FROZEN CHOPPED SPINACH, thawed and squeezed dry

½ cup/70 g finely diced WALLA WALLA OR OTHER SWEET ONION

1 tsp finely minced GARLIC

Grated zest of 1 large LEMON

2 tsp minced FRESH OREGANO leaves

½ cup/120 ml REDUCED-FAT MAYONNAISE

½ cup/120 ml REDUCED-FAT SOUR CREAM

1 cup/125 g crumbled FAT-FREE FETA CHEESE

1 tbsp FRESH LEMON JUICE

1 tsp KOSHER OR SEA SALT

½ tsp FRESHLY GROUND PEPPER

SKINNY DIPPERS: Baked Pita Chips, Crostini, Bruschetta, Baked Bagel Chips, slices of fresh baguette

1. Preheat the oven to 400°F/200°C/gas 6. Position a rack in the center of the oven. Have ready a 1-qt/1-L shallow baking dish.

2. In a medium bowl, mix together the spinach, onion, garlic, lemon zest, and oregano until well combined. Add the mayonnaise, sour cream, feta cheese, lemon juice, salt, and pepper. Stir until well combined. Taste and adjust the seasoning. Transfer to the baking dish and cover with aluminum foil. Bake until heated through, 25 to 30 minutes. Stir to fluff up the dip, and serve warm.

DIP DO-AHEAD: This dip can be prepared, covered, and refrigerated up to 1 day in advance. Remove from the refrigerator 40 minutes before baking.

MAKES
about

3

cups
(720 ml)

SERVING SIZE

2

tbsp

CALORIES	43
FAT	2.3 g
SAT	0.7 g
MONO	0.2 g
POLY	0.1 g
PROTEIN	3 g
CARB	2 g
FIBER	1 g
CHOL	5 mg
IRON	0.4 mg
SODIUM	189 mg
CALC	65.1 mg

Three-Cheese Pepperoncini Dip

Make this dip for a potluck or a casual event—backyard party, tailgating party, sports get-together—where there is a lot of grazing rather than an appetizer course followed by a main-course meal. I say that because this dip, though still light, is boldly flavored and filling. It's a no-brainer to pair this cheesy, spicy concoction with baked potato chips or a selection of crisp veggies, but the dip is creamy deliciousness when the dunkers include the Roasted Fingerling Potatoes on page 125.

½ cup/120 ml REDUCED-FAT SOUR CREAM

2 oz/72 g LOW-FAT CREAM CHEESE (bar style), at room temperature

1 container (16 oz/455 g) REDUCED-FAT COTTAGE CHEESE

½ cup/60 g drained, stemmed, and finely chopped PEPPERONCINI

2 tbsp minced FRESH FLAT-LEAF PARSLEY

Grated zest of ½ LEMON

½ tsp GARLIC POWDER

½ tsp KOSHER OR SEA SALT

SKINNY DIPPERS: Roasted Fingerling Potatoes, Baked Pita Chips, Crudités, baked potato chips

In the workbowl of a food processor fitted with the metal blade, process the sour cream and cream cheese until smooth. Scrape down the sides of the bowl once or twice until thoroughly combined. Add the cottage cheese, pepperoncini, parsley, lemon zest, garlic powder, and salt. Pulse several times to combine. The dip should be chunky, not smooth. Taste and adjust the seasoning. Transfer to a serving bowl and serve immediately.

DIP DO-AHEAD: This dip can be prepared up to 2 days in advance. Cover and refrigerate. Remove from the refrigerator 30 minutes before serving.

MAKES
about

2¼

cups
(540 ml)

SERVING SIZE

2

tbsp

CALORIES	43
FAT	2.2 g
SAT	1.2 g
MONO	0.5 g
POLY	0.1 g
PROTEIN	4 g
CARB	2 g
FIBER	0 g
CHOL	7 mg
IRON	0.1 mg
SODIUM	194 mg
CALC	36 mg

CALORIES	58
FAT	2.3 g
SAT	1.2 g
MONO	0.8 g
POLY	0.1 g
PROTEIN	4 g
CARB	7 g
FIBER	1 g
CHOL	7 mg
IRON	0.7 mg
SODIUM	169 mg
CALC	102 mg

Baked Mozzarella Marinara Spread

Think of a cheese pizza baked in a wood-fired oven and you'll understand why this spread is a crowd pleaser. Slather this baked marinara spread, which is topped with bubbly, cheesy mozzarella, on bruschetta or crostini for a warm, big-flavored appetizer. The tomato sauce is slow cooked, chock full of mellowed onions and garlic, given a kick of crushed red pepper, and finished with an herbal infusion of fresh basil.

1 tsp EXTRA-VIRGIN OLIVE OIL

1½ cups/200 g minced WALLA WALLA OR OTHER SWEET ONION

1 tbsp minced GARLIC

1½ tsp SUGAR

1 can (14.5 oz/415 g) CRUSHED TOMATOES in thick purée

½ cup/120 ml WATER

¼ cup/60 ml TOMATO PASTE/TOMATO PURÉE

1½ tsp CRUSHED RED PEPPER

1½ tbsp finely minced FRESH BASIL LEAVES

¼ cup/30 g freshly grated PARMESAN CHEESE, preferably Parmigiano-Reggiano

¾ cup/85 g shredded REDUCED-FAT MOZZARELLA CHEESE

SKINNY DIPPERS: Bruschetta, Herbed Cheddar Cheese Straws, Crostini, Grilled Japanese Eggplant, slices of fresh baguette

1. In a 10-in/25-cm nonstick sauté pan, heat the oil over medium-low heat. Add the onion, garlic, and sugar. Sauté, stirring frequently, until the onion glistens and begins to soften, about 4 minutes. Add the crushed tomatoes, including any juice from the can, along with the water, tomato paste/tomato purée, and crushed red pepper. Bring to a simmer, stirring frequently. Adjust the heat to low and cook, uncovered, stirring occasionally, until the tomato mixture is thick, about 45 minutes. Add the basil and Parmesan and continue to cook, stirring occasionally, another 5 minutes. Remove from the heat. Transfer to an oven-to-table, 1-qt/1-L shallow baking dish.

2. Position an oven rack about 4 in/10 cm below the heat source and preheat the broiler/grill. Scatter the mozzarella cheese evenly over the marinara spread. Broil/grill until the cheese bubbles and is beginning to brown, about 1 minute. Serve immediately.

DIP DO-AHEAD: The spread, without the mozzarella topping, can be prepared, covered, and refrigerated up to 2 days in advance. Remove from the refrigerator 40 minutes before serving. Heat the spread in a small saucepan or in the microwave until hot. Scatter the mozzarella over the top and broil/grill just before serving.

CALORIES	49
FAT	3.2 g
SAT	1.6 g
MONO	1 g
POLY	0.2 g
PROTEIN	3 g
CARB	2 g
FIBER	0 g
CHOL	9 mg
IRON	0.1 mg
SODIUM	114 mg
CALC	123 mg

Chorizo Chile Con Queso Lite

This dip is packed with chunks of spicy-hot chorizo, punctuated with fire-roasted chiles, and speckled with bits of fresh tomato. The cheese, of course, isn't sliced from a boxed loaf; it's a flavorful, reduced-fat Mexican cheese blend.

2 oz/55 g bulk PORK CHORIZO (see page 13)

½ cup/70 g diced WHITE ONION

1 cup/192 g diced FRESH TOMATO

2 ANAHEIM CHILES, diced (see page 16)

1 tbsp diced canned CHIPOTLE CHILES IN ADOBO (see page 13)

2 cups/225 g shredded REDUCED-FAT MEXICAN CHEESE BLEND

1 cup/240 ml LOW-FAT (1%) MILK

2 tbsp REDUCED-FAT SOUR CREAM

2 tbsp thinly sliced GREEN/SPRING ONIONS, including green tops

2 tbsp chopped CILANTRO/FRESH CORIANDER LEAVES

SKINNY DIPPERS: Baked Tortilla Chips, Roasted Fingerling Potatoes, crusty peasant bread, baked potato chips, taro root chips

1. In a 3-qt/3-L saucepan over medium heat, sauté the chorizo, stirring constantly and using the side of a spatula to break up the chunks, until cooked through, about 3 minutes. Add the onion, tomato, and both varieties of chiles. Sauté, stirring frequently, until the onion softens, about 3 minutes. Turn the heat to medium-low and add the cheese, stirring constantly, until the cheese melts, about 2 minutes. Add the milk and sour cream and stir until heated through. Stir in the green/spring onions and cilantro/fresh coriander.

2. Transfer to a fondue pot set over an alcohol or Sterno flame to keep warm. Serve immediately.

DIP DO-AHEAD: This dip can be prepared 1 day in advance. Let cool, transfer it to a covered container, and refrigerate. Reheat in a sauce-pan and then transfer to a fondue pot for serving.

SERVING SIZE

2

tbsp

CALORIES	59
FAT	3.4 g
SAT	2.2 g
MONO	0.9 g
POLY	0.1 g
PROTEIN	5 g
CARB	1 g
FIBER	0 g
CHOL	10 mg
IRON	0.1 mg
SODIUM	141 mg
CALC	171 mg

Microbrew Cheddar Cheese Spread

Portland, Oregon, where I live, has established itself as the unofficial microbrew capital of America. (Some might argue otherwise, but the smell of hops as you drive around town is undeniable.) There are more than thirty breweries in the metropolitan area and at least sixty-three in the state. With so many good brews to choose from, it made sense to create a cheese spread for the book that lightened up on the fat content but didn't skimp on the fresh, floral flavors of a good amber ale. I made this spread with Widmer's Drop Top, a favorite amber. Find one you like, because this recipe only uses about ½ cup/120 ml of beer—which leaves the rest for drinking.

2½ cups/225 g shredded REDUCED-FAT CHEDDAR CHEESE

2 tbsp minced SHALLOTS

2 tsp minced GARLIC

1 tsp whole-grain DIJON MUSTARD

½ tsp extra-hot HORSERADISH

7 to 8 tbsp/100 to 120 ml AMBER ALE

1 tbsp snipped FRESH CHIVES for garnish

SKINNY DIPPERS: Marbled Rye Toasts, Baked Pita Chips, Crostini, pretzel thins

In the workbowl of a food processor fitted with the metal blade, process the cheese, shallots, garlic, mustard, and horseradish until they form a coarse paste. With the machine running, pour the ale through the feed tube and process until creamy. Scrape down the sides of the bowl once or twice until thoroughly combined. Transfer to a serving bowl. Cover and refrigerate for at least 2 hours to allow the flavors to meld. Remove from the refrigerator 1 hour before serving. Garnish with the chives.

DIP DO-AHEAD: This dip can be prepared up to 1 day in advance. Cover and refrigerate.

Roasted Red Pepper & Goat Cheese Ranch Dip

MAKES
about

$1\frac{1}{2}$

cups
(360 ml)

SERVING SIZE

2

tbsp

CALORIES	53
FAT	4 g
SAT	2.2 g
MONO	0.9 g
POLY	0.5 g
PROTEIN	3 g
CARB	1 g
FIBER	0 g
CHOL	7 mg
IRON	0.3 mg
SODIUM	103 mg
CALC	28 mg

Until a few years ago, I had no idea how many people love ranch dressing, but then I was asked to develop recipes for Hidden Valley Ranch, and my ranch-loving friends came out of the closet. Given the popularity of that classic ranch flavor, it made perfect sense to include a ranch dip in this book. Sure enough, everyone who samples this dip goes back for second, third, and fourth dunks. You can serve the dip with chips, but it is especially good with crudités.

⅓ cup/75 ml jarred ROASTED RED PEPPERS/CAPSICUMS, drained but not blotted dry

6 oz/170 g soft GOAT'S MILK CHEESE, at room temperature

1½ tsp HIDDEN VALLEY RANCH BUTTERMILK SALAD DRESSING & SEASONING MIX

4½ tbsp/70 ml REDUCED-FAT BUTTERMILK

3 tbsp snipped FRESH CHIVES

SKINNY DIPPERS: Crudités, Roasted Cauliflower

In the workbowl of a food processor fitted with the metal blade, process the peppers/capsicums, cheese, and seasoning mix until smooth, scraping down the sides of the workbowl once or twice, until well blended. With the machine running, pour the buttermilk through the feed tube and process until combined. Transfer the dip to a serving bowl and stir in the chives. Cover and refrigerate for at least 8 hours or overnight to allow the flavors to meld. Remove from the refrigerator just before serving.

DIP DO-AHEAD: This dip can be prepared up to 2 days in advance. Cover and refrigerate.

Date & Blue Cheese Ball

Cheese balls were all the rage in the 1970s, an easy, tasty, fab party food for any occasion. What's old is now retro-chic—this lightened-up cheese ball seduces with the sweetness of dates, the savory bite of blue cheese, a hint of shallot, and a teasing whiff of lemon zest.

8 oz/225 g of LOW-FAT CREAM CHEESE (bar style), at room temperature

1 cup/115 g crumbled BLUE CHEESE, at room temperature

1 tbsp REDUCED-FAT BUTTERMILK

3 tbsp minced MEDJOOL DATES (5 or 6 pitted dates)

1 tbsp minced SHALLOTS

1 tsp grated LEMON ZEST

1/4 tsp KOSHER OR SEA SALT

1/4 tsp FRESHLY GROUND PEPPER

2 tbsp minced FRESH FLAT-LEAF PARSLEY

2 1/2 tbsp finely chopped toasted WALNUTS (see page 18)

SKINNY DIPPERS: Crostini, Baked Pita Chips, Baked Bagel Chips, Marbled Rye Toasts, celery and carrot sticks

1. In the bowl of a stand mixer fitted with the paddle attachment, beat together the cream cheese, blue cheese, and buttermilk on medium speed until smooth and creamy, about 2 minutes. Add the dates, shallots, lemon zest, salt, and pepper and beat until well combined.

2. Transfer the cheese mixture to a large sheet of plastic wrap/cling film and form it into a ball. Wrap the ball in the wrap/film and refrigerate until well chilled, at least 2 hours or overnight.

3. In a shallow bowl or plate, mix together the parsley and walnuts. Remove the cheese ball from the refrigerator. With the wrap/film still on, shape into a well-formed ball. Unwrap the cheese mixture and roll it gently in the nut mixture until all sides are well covered. Serve immediately or cover and refrigerate until ready to serve.

DIP DO-AHEAD: The cheese ball can be prepared up to 2 days in advance. Cover and refrigerate.

MAKES about

1 1/2

cups
(360 ml)

SERVING SIZE

2

tbsp

CALORIES	59
FAT	3.9 g
SAT	2.1 g
MONO	1 g
POLY	0.4 g
PROTEIN	2 g
CARB	4 g
FIBER	0 g
CHOL	10 mg
IRON	0.1 mg
SODIUM	109 mg
CALC	41 mg

CHAPTER 4

Bean and Legume Dips

Substantial, nutritious, and loaded with fiber and protein, these bean and legume dips take you on a flavor journey through America, Mexico, Italy, and the Middle East. Intriguing spices accent a variety of beans, from cannellini and chickpeas to the triple play of pinto, kidney, and pinquito beans. Springtime favorites from the farmers' market—fresh fava/broad beans, dandelion greens, and garlic scapes—bring color and vibrancy to classic dips. This chapter is filled with one-dip wonders.

SERVING SIZE

2

tbsp

CALORIES	54
FAT	3.5 g
SAT	0.5 g
MONO	2.5 g
POLY	0.4 g
PROTEIN	2 g
CARB	4 g
FIBER	1 g
CHOL	0 mg
IRON	0.4 mg
SODIUM	110 mg
CALC	8.9 mg

Fresh Fava Bean Dip

In the springtime, when the farmers' market has bushels of fava/broad beans, I buy a huge bagful and take some lazy time to remove the beans from their inedible pods. Once that is done, this sensational dip, with a kick of lemon and gentle whiff of garlic, is a breeze to make.

2 lb/910 g FAVA/BROAD BEANS, shelled (about 2 cups shelled beans)

1½ tsp KOSHER OR SEA SALT

1 large clove GARLIC

½ tsp FRESHLY GROUND PEPPER

¼ tsp SUGAR

2 tsp minced FRESH THYME LEAVES

4 tbsp/60 ml EXTRA-VIRGIN OLIVE OIL

1½ tbsp FRESH LEMON JUICE

1 tbsp WATER

SKINNY DIPPERS: Bruschetta, Crostini, Baked Pita Chips, Baked Wonton Crisps, slices of fresh baguette

1. Fill a 3-qt/3-L saucepan two-thirds full of water and bring to a boil over high heat. Add the fava/broad beans and 1 tsp of the salt, and cook until bright green and tender, 4 minutes. Drain in a colander, then rinse under cold water until cool. Using your fingertips, slip the beans from their tough skins, discarding the skins.

2. In the workbowl of a food processor fitted with the metal blade, process the garlic, the remaining ½ tsp of salt, the pepper, and sugar until the garlic is finely minced. Add the beans and thyme and process until the beans are finely chopped. Add the olive oil, lemon juice, and water and process until the mixture forms a coarse purée. Transfer to a serving bowl, cover, and set aside at room temperature for 30 minutes to allow the flavors to meld. Serve at room temperature.

DIP DO-AHEAD: This dip can be prepared up to 2 days in advance. Cover and refrigerate. Remove from the refrigerator 45 minutes before serving.

MAKES

1³/₄

cups
(420 ml)

SERVING SIZE

2

tbsp

CALORIES	56
FAT	3.4 g
SAT	0.4 g
MONO	2.2 g
POLY	0.5 g
PROTEIN	2 g
CARB	5 g
FIBER	1 g
CHOL	0 mg
IRON	0.5 mg
SODIUM	43 mg
CALC	10 mg

Hummus Lightened Up

Of course you can buy hummus in almost any grocery store nowadays, but why not make a delectable, fresher-tasting, healthier version— and save money to boot? With a food processor, it takes 1 minute of whizzing. Ideally, every ingredient in this recipe is a pantry staple— for me, that's what casual, spur-of-the-moment entertaining is all about.

2 cloves GARLIC

½ tsp KOSHER OR SEA SALT

⅛ tsp FRESHLY GROUND PEPPER

1 can (15 oz/430 g) CHICKPEAS, drained and rinsed

3 tbsp EXTRA-VIRGIN OLIVE OIL, plus more for drizzling

2 tbsp FRESH LEMON JUICE

1 tbsp WATER

Sprinkle of PAPRIKA

2 tsp finely diced RED BELL PEPPER/CAPSICUM

SKINNY DIPPERS: Baked Pita Chips, warmed wedges of fresh pita, Crudités, Baked Bagel Chips

In the workbowl of a food processor fitted with the metal blade, process the garlic, salt, and pepper until the garlic is finely minced. Scrape down the sides of the bowl, add the chickpeas, and process until the beans are finely mashed. Add the 3 tbsp olive oil, lemon juice, and water and process until the mixture is puréed. Taste and adjust the seasoning. Transfer to a shallow serving bowl and garnish the top, first with a drizzle of olive oil, then a sprinkle of paprika; finish by scattering the diced bell pepper/capsicum over top. Serve at room temperature.

DIP DO-AHEAD: This dip can be prepared up to 2 days in advance. Cover and refrigerate. Remove from the refrigerator 45 minutes before serving.

Herbed Hummus bi Tahini

This dip, a variation on what you might know as hummus, is a traditional Lebanese spread served with pita bread. Select one of the suggested fresh herbs for an extra hit of fresh flavor, then add in a big kick of garlic to brighten the softer, subtle taste of tahini. Smooth and creamy, this dip is best when made using a food processor. Make it a couple of hours ahead of serving time so the flavors have time to meld.

2 cloves GARLIC

¾ tsp KOSHER OR SEA SALT

1 can (15 oz/430 g) CHICKPEAS, drained and rinsed

½ cup/120 ml FRESH LEMON JUICE

3 tbsp TAHINI (see page 15)

2 tbsp minced FRESH FLAT-LEAF PARSLEY, THYME, BASIL, OR CILANTRO/FRESH CORIANDER

SKINNY DIPPERS: Baked Pita Chips, Crudités, warmed wedges of fresh pita, Baked Bagel Chips

In the workbowl of a food processor fitted with the metal blade, process the garlic and salt until the garlic is finely minced. Scrape down the sides of the bowl, add the chickpeas, and process until the beans are finely mashed. Add the lemon juice and tahini. Process the mixture until smooth and puréed. Taste and adjust the seasoning. Add a tablespoon or two of water if the hummus is too thick. Scatter the herbs over the top and pulse just until they are incorporated. Transfer to a shallow serving bowl. Cover and set aside for 2 hours to allow the flavors to meld.

DIP DO-AHEAD: This dip can be prepared up to 2 days in advance. Cover and refrigerate. Remove from the refrigerator 45 minutes before serving.

MAKES
about
2
cups
(480 ml)

SERVING SIZE
2
tbsp

CALORIES	45
FAT	1.9 g
SAT	0.3 g
MONO	0.7 g
POLY	0.8 g
PROTEIN	2 g
CARB	6 g
FIBER	1 g
CHOL	0 mg
IRON	0.7 mg
SODIUM	77 mg
CALC	21 mg

Curry Pumpkin Hummus

Seeking to broaden the flavor profile of hummus beyond the bounds of Middle Eastern tradition, I've combined pumpkin and chickpeas and added an underlying current of spice, a little sweetness, and a touch of lusty garlic. This dip is perfect for autumn entertaining.

1 tbsp EXTRA-VIRGIN OLIVE OIL

2 cloves GARLIC, minced

1 tbsp CURRY POWDER

1½ tbsp HONEY

1 can (15 oz/430 g) CHICKPEAS, drained and rinsed

1 can (15 oz/430 g) UNSWEETENED PUMPKIN PURÉE

1½ tsp finely minced FRESH GINGER

1½ tsp KOSHER OR SEA SALT

TOASTED PUMPKIN SEEDS (see page 18), optional

SKINNY DIPPERS: Baked Pita Chips, Baked Bagel Chips, Baked Wonton Crisps, Herbed Cheddar Cheese Straws, Crostini, Bruschetta, Roasted Cauliflower, warmed wedges of fresh pita

1. In a small nonstick frying pan over medium heat, warm the oil and swirl to coat the pan. Add the garlic and sauté just until beginning to soften, about 30 seconds. Add the curry powder and sauté, stirring constantly, until fragrant, about 1 minute longer. Stir in the honey, remove from the heat, and set aside.

2. In the workbowl of a food processor fitted with the metal blade, process the chickpeas until finely mashed. Add the pumpkin purée, ginger, salt, and the garlic mixture. Process until the hummus is smooth and puréed. Taste and adjust the seasoning. Transfer to a serving bowl. Cover and set aside for 1 hour to allow the flavors to meld. Garnish with toasted pumpkin seeds, if desired.

DIP DO-AHEAD: This dip can be prepared up to 2 days in advance. Cover and refrigerate. Remove from the refrigerator 45 minutes before serving.

MAKES

2³⁄₄

cups
(660 ml)

SERVING SIZE

2

tbsp

CALORIES	36
FAT	1 g
SAT	0.1 g
MONO	0.5 g
POLY	0.2 g
PROTEIN	1 g
CARB	6 g
FIBER	2 g
CHOL	0 mg
IRON	0.7 mg
SODIUM	126 mg
CALC	13 mg

CALORIES	71
FAT	2.7 g
SAT	0.4 g
MONO	1.9 g
POLY	0.3 g
PROTEIN	3 g
CARB	9 g
FIBER	2 g
CHOL	0 mg
IRON	1.3 mg
SODIUM	75 mg
CALC	33 mg

White Bean Dip
with Garlic Scapes

Garlic scapes, a farmers' market shopper's delight, are the curled flower stalks that shoot up from the garlic bulb. Growers cut them off to encourage better bulb growth. Look for vividly green, skinny stalks—some straight, some curled—which often have a tightly closed bud. Scapes have a pronounced crunch and a mild garlic flavor. I snip them and use them in salads, cut them into 2-in/5-cm lengths and stir-fry them, or blanch them to use in soups. Stirred into this velvety bean dip, the scapes add flecks of bright color and a mild garlicky bite.

2 cans (15 oz/430 g each) CANNELLINI BEANS, drained and rinsed

3 tbsp EXTRA-VIRGIN OLIVE OIL

3 tbsp FRESH LEMON JUICE

1 to 3 tbsp WATER

3/4 tsp KOSHER OR SEA SALT

FRESHLY GROUND PEPPER

1/2 cup/50 g finely sliced GARLIC SCAPES

SKINNY DIPPERS: Crudités, Baked Pita Chips, Crostini, Bruschetta, Baked Bagel Chips, Grilled Japanese Eggplant

In the workbowl of a food processor fitted with the metal blade, process the beans until mashed. Add the olive oil, lemon juice, 1 tbsp of the water, the salt, and a few grinds of pepper. Process until puréed and smooth, adding additional water until the spread is smooth and creamy. Scatter the garlic scapes over the top and pulse just until incorporated. Taste and adjust the seasoning. Transfer to a serving bowl and serve immediately.

DIP DO-AHEAD: This dip can be prepared up to 2 days in advance. Cover and refrigerate. Remove from the refrigerator 20 minutes before serving.

CALORIES	50
FAT	0.7 g
SAT	0.4 g
MONO	0.2 g
POLY	0.1 g
PROTEIN	3 g
CARB	8 g
FIBER	2 g
CHOL	1 mg
IRON	0.7 mg
SODIUM	87 mg
CALC	20 mg

Three-Bean Dip

I was perusing the prepared dips at my local grocery store and came across an organic, locally made three-bean dip. It wasn't particularly flavorful or interesting. At play in my kitchen—as I think of the time I spend developing recipes—I started experimenting. Here's my version of a three-bean dip, colorfully dotted with cilantro/fresh coriander and layered with feisty flavors.

1 cup/135 g chopped WHITE ONION

1 JALAPEÑO CHILE, seeds and ribs removed, chopped (see page 16)

2 tsp finely chopped GARLIC

2 tsp KOSHER OR SEA SALT

1 can (15 oz/430 g) PINTO BEANS, drained and rinsed

1 can (15 oz/430 g) KIDNEY BEANS, drained and rinsed

1 can (15 oz/430 g) PINQUITO BEANS, drained and rinsed

3½ tbsp FRESH LIME JUICE

2 tbsp APPLE CIDER VINEGAR

¾ tsp CHILI POWDER

½ tsp GROUND CUMIN

½ cup/120 ml REDUCED-FAT SOUR CREAM

¼ cup/15 g minced CILANTRO/FRESH CORIANDER LEAVES

SKINNY DIPPERS: Baked Tortilla Chips, Baked Pita Chips, Roasted Fingerling Potatoes, baked potato chips

In the workbowl of a food processor fitted with the metal blade, process the onion, jalapeño, garlic, and salt until finely minced. Add all the beans, the lime juice, vinegar, chili powder, and cumin and purée until smooth. Add the sour cream and cilantro/fresh coriander and pulse until combined. Taste and adjust the seasoning. Transfer to a serving bowl, cover, and set aside at room temperature for 30 minutes to allow the flavors to meld.

DIP DO-AHEAD: This dip can be prepared up to 2 days in advance. Cover and refrigerate. Remove from the refrigerator 45 minutes before serving.

Chipotle Black Bean Dip

Layers of flavor make this dip a hearty, healthful favorite. The complex taste comes from simmering the green/spring onions and spices with the beans and adding smoky chipotle chiles in adobo. Serve this dip during a sports party when game watchers need sustenance.

1½ tbsp CANOLA OIL

½ cup/120 ml thinly sliced GREEN/SPRING ONIONS, including green tops

2 tsp GROUND CORIANDER

2 tsp GROUND CUMIN

2 cans (15 oz/430 g each) BLACK BEANS, drained and rinsed

⅓ cup/75 ml WATER

¼ cup/60 ml freshly squeezed LIME JUICE

2 tsp diced canned CHIPOTLE CHILES IN ADOBO (see page 13)

2 tsp KOSHER OR SEA SALT

½ cup/120 ml REDUCED-FAT SOUR CREAM

½ cup/30 g plus 1 tbsp minced CILANTRO/FRESH CORIANDER LEAVES

SKINNY DIPPERS: Baked Tortilla Chips, Baked Pita Chips, baked potato chips

1. In a 10-in/25-cm nonstick sauté pan, heat the oil over medium heat. Add the onions, ground coriander, and cumin. Sauté, stirring frequently, until the onions are softened, about 2 minutes. Add the beans and water. Simmer until the water evaporates, 5 to 7 minutes. Cool in the pan for 5 minutes.

2. In the workbowl of a food processor fitted with the metal blade, process the bean mixture until coarsely mashed. Add the lime juice, chipotle chiles, and salt. Process until smooth and puréed. Add the sour cream and ½ cup/120 ml of the cilantro/fresh coriander. Pulse just until the cilantro is incorporated. Taste and adjust the seasoning. Transfer to a serving bowl. Garnish with the remaining cilantro and serve immediately.

DIP DO-AHEAD: This dip can be prepared up to 2 days in advance. Cover and refrigerate. Remove from the refrigerator 45 minutes before serving.

MAKES
about

2½

cups
(600 ml)

SERVING SIZE

2

tbsp

CALORIES	57
FAT	2.1 g
SAT	0.6 g
MONO	1 g
POLY	0.4 g
PROTEIN	3 g
CARB	7 g
FIBER	2 g
CHOL	2 mg
IRON	0.8 mg
SODIUM	164 mg
CALC	21 mg

Red Lentil & Roasted Garlic Spread

MAKES

2

cups
(480 ml)

SERVING SIZE

2

tbsp

Quick-cooking, tender red lentils take on deep garlic flavor in this dip, which is punched up with a mouth-puckering dose of lemon juice, a subtle infusion of cumin, and a double blast of chili powder and hot pepper sauce.

CALORIES	60
FAT	2 g
SAT	0.3 g
MONO	1.3 g
POLY	0.3 g
PROTEIN	3 g
CARB	8 g
FIBER	1 g
CHOL	0 mg
IRON	1.1 mg
SODIUM	117 mg
CALC	10 mg

1 cup/185 g RED LENTILS

1²/₃ cups/405 ml WATER

6 large cloves ROASTED GARLIC (see page 17)

¼ cup/60 ml FRESH LEMON JUICE

2 tbsp ROASTED-GARLIC OLIVE OIL (see page 14)

1½ tsp KOSHER OR SEA SALT

1½ tsp GROUND CUMIN

1 tsp CHILI POWDER

½ tsp HOT SAUCE, such as Tabasco

SKINNY DIPPERS: Crudités, Baked Pita Chips, Spice-Coated Pita Chips, Baked Bagel Chips, Roasted Garlic Bagel Chips

1. Place the lentils and water in a small saucepan and bring the water to a boil over high heat. Boil for 3 minutes and then remove the pan from the heat. Cover and let stand for 12 minutes. (The lentils will have absorbed almost all the water.)

2. Using a slotted spoon, transfer the lentils to the workbowl of a food processor fitted with the metal blade and reserve any liquid remaining in the pan. Add the roasted garlic, lemon juice, olive oil, salt, cumin, chili powder, and hot sauce and process until puréed. Add a tablespoon or two of the reserved lentil cooking liquid if the dip isn't creamy and smooth. Taste and add more salt, if desired. Transfer to a serving bowl and serve immediately.

DIP DO-AHEAD: This dip can be prepared up to 3 days in advance. Cover and refrigerate. Remove from the refrigerator 20 minutes before serving.

SERVING SIZE

2
tbsp

CALORIES	42
FAT	1.3 g
SAT	0.7 g
MONO	0.3 g
POLY	0.1 g
PROTEIN	2 g
CARB	6 g
FIBER	2 g
CHOL	3 mg
IRON	0.6 mg
SODIUM	91 mg
CALC	20 mg

Poblano
Black-Eyed Pea Dip

Let's mix up cultural traditions by taking black-eyed peas, a popular Southern legume, and flavoring them with roasted poblano chiles—the dark, almost black, richly flavored green chile from central Mexico. What you have is a party dip with a winning flavor combination accented with a touch of onion, a wisp of garlic, the tang of sour cream, and the charm of cilantro/fresh coriander.

2 medium POBLANO CHILES, roasted (see page 16)

1 can (15.5 oz/445 g) BLACK-EYED PEAS, drained and rinsed

¼ cup/35 g diced WALLA WALLA OR OTHER SWEET ONION

2 tsp minced GARLIC

¾ tsp KOSHER OR SEA SALT

¼ tsp FRESHLY GROUND PEPPER

½ cup/120 ml REDUCED-FAT SOUR CREAM

2 tbsp chopped CILANTRO/FRESH CORIANDER LEAVES

SKINNY DIPPERS: Baked Tortilla Chips, Baked Pita Chips, Crostini, baked potato chips

In the workbowl of a food processor fitted with the metal blade, process the chiles until finely chopped. Add the black-eyed peas, onion, garlic, salt, and pepper. Process until puréed. Add the sour cream and process until combined. Stir in 1 tbsp of the cilantro/fresh coriander. Pulse just until the cilantro is incorporated. Taste and adjust the seasoning. Transfer to a serving bowl. Garnish with the remaining cilantro and serve immediately.

DIP DO-AHEAD: This dip can be prepared up to 2 days in advance. Cover and refrigerate. Remove from the refrigerator 20 minutes before serving.

Italian Fava Bean Purée with Dandelion Greens

Dried fava/broad beans are meaty, nutty, and incredibly flavorful, as well as a powerhouse of protein, fiber, and iron. This coarse purée, topped with wilted greens, is a classic throughout southern Italy. I used red-stemmed dandelion greens from the farmers' market to top this dip, but you could use other greens such as Swiss chard, curly endive, broccoli rabe (also known as rapini), or beet greens. Traditionally, the purée is swirled in the bowl to create a few moats that can hold a spoonful of olive oil; I skip this final flourish in order to keep the dip skinny, but you're welcome to drizzle a little extra-virgin olive oil on top.

1⅓ cups/225 g dried, peeled FAVA/BROAD BEANS

2 large cloves GARLIC, peeled but left whole

1 tbsp FRESH THYME LEAVES

2 tsp KOSHER OR SEA SALT

4 tbsp/60 ml EXTRA-VIRGIN OLIVE OIL

4 cups/140 g coarsely chopped DANDELION GREENS

¼ tsp CRUSHED RED PEPPER

FRESHLY GROUND PEPPER

SKINNY DIPPERS: Bruschetta, Crostini

1. Place the fava/broad beans in a medium bowl, cover with water to a depth of 2 in/5 cm, and allow the beans to soak overnight.

CONTINUED »

MAKES
about

2½

cups
(600 ml)

SERVING SIZE

2

tbsp

CALORIES	48
FAT	2.8 g
SAT	0.4 g
MONO	2 g
POLY	0.3 g
PROTEIN	2 g
CARB	4 g
FIBER	1 g
CHOL	0 mg
IRON	0.6 mg
SODIUM	108 mg
CALC	28 mg

2. Drain the beans and transfer them to a 4-qt/4-L saucepan. Add 5 cups/1.2 L of water, along with the garlic and thyme. Partially cover the pot and bring the beans to a boil over medium-high heat. Reduce the heat to low and cook the beans, partially covered, at a bare simmer for 15 minutes. Add 1 tsp of the salt and continue to cook, partially covered, stirring occasionally, until the beans are very soft and partially broken down and can be easily mashed, about 1½ hours. (Check the water level from time to time. Add a little more water, if necessary.)

3. Remove from the heat. Drain the beans, reserving the cooking liquid. Using a food mill or a potato masher, finely mash the beans. Stir in 3 tbsp of the olive oil and ½ tsp of the salt. Add a tablespoon or so of the reserved cooking liquid, if needed, to give the purée a spreadable consistency. Taste and adjust the seasoning. Transfer to a shallow serving dish and set aside.

4. In a 10-in/25-cm sauté pan, preferably nonstick, heat the remaining 1 tbsp of olive oil over medium heat. Swirl to coat the pan and add the dandelion greens. Sauté, stirring constantly, until the greens are wilted and tender, about 4 minutes. Season with the remaining ½ tsp of salt, the crushed red pepper, and a little ground pepper. Arrange the greens in the center of the fava bean purée and serve immediately.

DIP DO-AHEAD: This dip can be prepared up to 1 day in advance. Remove from the refrigerator 1 hour before serving. The greens can be cleaned, chopped, wrapped in paper towels/absorbent paper and placed inside a lock-top plastic bag up to 1 day in advance. The greens are best when sautéed within 1 hour of serving.

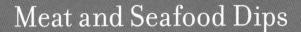

5

Meat and Seafood Dips

Give a "stealth health" protein boost to a party by serving a meat or seafood dip. Seafood and meat are good sources of protein, especially fish that are rich in omega-3 fatty acids, such as wild salmon and albacore tuna. Big, meaty flavor is packed into the Tex-Mex Hot Beef Chili Dip on page 106, yet only ½ pound/225 grams of extra-lean ground/minced beef is used, and it acts almost like a condiment. The fat won't be missed in the shamelessly rich smoked salmon pâté, which is more typically made with full-fat cream cheese and whipping cream. And party on while slimming down with morsels of shrimp lustily combined with ginger and garlic in the Skinny Shrimp Dip on page 111. These are dynamic dips with shapely results.

MAKES

$2^1/_2$

cups
(600 ml)

SERVING SIZE

2

tbsp

CALORIES	47
FAT	0.6 g
SAT	0.2 g
MONO	0 g
POLY	0.1 g
PROTEIN	3 g
CARB	7 g
FIBER	2 g
CHOL	2 mg
IRON	0.7 mg
SODIUM	121 mg
CALC	25 mg

Slimmed-Down Bacon & Bean Dip

Trimming calories and reducing fat while still delivering big flavor takes some creativity and determination. A warm bacon, onion, and garlic–fueled bean dip that I tasted at a party was my inspiration for this recipe, but I needed to find a way to cut the fat. My well-stocked grocery store had a product I hadn't seen before—reduced-fat bacon. Once I had diced the bacon, sautéed it until crisp, and then blotted it on paper towels/absorbent paper to remove excess fat, I was able to slim the dip and pack on flavor. That's a swine decision!

6 strips (5 oz/140 g) lean 25%-LESS-FAT BACON/STREAKY BACON, diced

2 cups/270 g finely chopped WALLA WALLA OR OTHER SWEET ONION

2 tbsp minced GARLIC

2 tsp CRUSHED RED PEPPER

2 tbsp chopped FRESH THYME LEAVES

6 tbsp/90 ml SHERRY VINEGAR

2 cans (15.5 oz/445 g each) GREAT NORTHERN WHITE BEANS, drained and rinsed

½ cup/120 ml LOW-SODIUM, 99%-FAT-FREE BEEF BROTH

½ cup/120 ml WATER

1½ tsp KOSHER OR SEA SALT

1 tsp grated LEMON ZEST

SKINNY DIPPERS: Baked Tortilla Chips, Crudités, Baked Pita Chips, baked potato chips

1. In a 10-in/25-cm nonstick frying pan over medium heat, cook the bacon/streaky bacon until it is crisp and all the fat is rendered. Using a slotted spoon, transfer the bacon to a plate lined with a double thickness of paper towels/absorbent paper. Blot the bacon to remove excess fat. Set aside.

2. Drain all but 1 tsp of the bacon fat from the frying pan. Return the frying pan to medium heat and add the onion. Sauté, stirring frequently, until soft but not brown, about 5 minutes. Add the garlic and crushed red pepper. Continue to sauté the onion, stirring frequently, until light golden brown, about 15 minutes. Adjust the heat to medium low, if necessary. Add the thyme and cooked bacon to the pan and stir for 30 seconds. Pour the vinegar over the top and simmer, stirring occasionally, until the liquid is reduced by two-thirds. Add the beans, beef broth, and water and simmer, stirring occasionally, until the liquid has reduced by two-thirds. Add the salt and lemon zest. Remove from the heat and let cool in the pan for 5 minutes.

3. Transfer the bean mixture to the workbowl of a food processor fitted with the metal blade. Pulse until the dip is spreadable but still has a chunky texture. Taste and adjust the seasoning. Transfer to a serving bowl and serve immediately.

DIP DO-AHEAD: This dip can be prepared up to 2 days in advance. Cover and refrigerate. Warm in a microwave or on the stovetop in a double boiler just before serving.

2½

cups
(600 ml)

SERVING SIZE

2

tbsp

CALORIES 57

....

FAT 3.3 g

SAT 1.2 g

MONO 1.5 g

POLY 0.3 g

....

PROTEIN 4 g

CARB 2 g

FIBER 0 g

CHOL 15 mg

IRON 0.3 mg

SODIUM 221 mg

CALC 9 mg

Thai-Style Spicy Pork Dip

Thai ingredients and cooking techniques create a mesmerizing dip layered with sweet, smoky, and pungent accents. You'll ratchet your cooking skills up a bit as the cherry tomatoes sizzle and char in one frying pan while the shallots, garlic, and Thai bird chiles blacken in another. Send any smoke through the hood above the stove and savor the intense flavors when these charred gems are puréed and blended into the cooked pork. Adding fish sauce, lime juice, and sugar as the combo simmers turns it into an irresistible dip with a backbeat of fiery heat. Reduce the number of chiles for a tamer, less spicy dip.

2 cups/355 g CHERRY TOMATOES

6 small SHALLOTS

5 THAI BIRD CHILES, stems removed (see page 16)

5 large cloves GARLIC

1 lb/455 g EXTRA-LEAN GROUND/MINCED PORK

½ cup/120 ml WATER

3 tbsp FISH SAUCE

1 tbsp FRESH LIME JUICE

1 tbsp SUGAR

....

SKINNY DIPPERS: Baked Wonton Crisps, Cucumber and Carrot Crudités, Belgian endive/chicory

1. In a 10-in/25-cm nonstick frying pan over medium heat, char the tomatoes, shaking the pan frequently, until the tomatoes are blackened on all sides but haven't burst, 8 to 10 minutes. Remove from the heat and set aside.

2. Meanwhile, in a second medium nonstick frying pan over medium heat, char the shallots, chiles, and garlic, shaking the pan frequently and turning the aromatics until evenly charred on all sides, about 5 minutes. (Remove the garlic and chiles to a plate as they blacken. They will char more quickly than the shallots.)

3. Transfer the warm tomatoes, shallots, chiles, and garlic to a food processor or blender and purée.

4. Using the same frying pan you blackened the tomatoes in, brown the pork over medium heat, breaking up the chunks of meat with the side of a heatproof spatula, until cooked through and no longer pink, 5 to 7 minutes. Using a slotted spoon, transfer the cooked pork to a plate lined with a double thickness of paper towels/absorbent paper. Wipe the frying pan clean, then return the pork to the frying pan. Add the tomato-chile purée, water, fish sauce, lime juice, and sugar. Increase the heat to medium-high and simmer the mixture until it thickens to a chunky, diplike consistency, about 10 minutes. Taste and adjust the seasoning. Transfer to a serving bowl and serve immediately.

DIP DO-AHEAD: This dip can be prepared up to 1 day in advance. Cool, cover, and refrigerate. Just before serving, heat until hot in a microwave or on the stovetop in a frying pan.

SERVING SIZE

¼

cup
(60 ml)

CALORIES   79
....
FAT   2.8 g
SAT   0.8 g
MONO   0.8 g
POLY   0.3 g
....
PROTEIN   6 g
CARB   8 g
FIBER   2 g
CHOL   12 mg
IRON   1.2 mg
SODIUM   249 mg
CALC   49 mg

Tex-Mex Hot Beef Chili Dip

Don't scan the long ingredient list and pass up this recipe because it looks too complicated—it isn't! Actually, it requires very little chopping, a few quick-to-measure spices, several cans to open, and just one pan. What is utterly amazing is the end result—a chunky, meaty chili dip, seasoned with a lip-buzzing blend of spices that is guaranteed to jump-start any casual get-together. Leftovers? Just eat them with a spoon.

1 tsp CANOLA OIL

1½ cups/200 g finely chopped YELLOW ONION

2 tbsp minced GARLIC

1½ tbsp KOSHER OR SEA SALT

8 oz/225 g EXTRA-LEAN GROUND/MINCED BEEF

1 tbsp CHILI POWDER

1 tsp DRIED OREGANO

1 tsp GROUND CUMIN

¼ tsp CAYENNE PEPPER

3 tbsp TOMATO PASTE/TOMATO PURÉE

½ cup/120 ml LOW-SODIUM, 99%-FAT-FREE BEEF BROTH

1 can (14.5 oz/415 g) DICED TOMATOES

½ cup/120 ml WATER

1 tsp SUGAR

1 can (15 oz/430 g) PINTO BEANS, drained and rinsed

3 tbsp seeded and minced JALAPEÑO CHILE (see page 16)

1 tbsp FRESH LIME JUICE

3 tbsp thinly sliced GREEN/SPRING ONION, including green tops, plus 2 tbsp for garnish

3 tbsp chopped CILANTRO/FRESH CORIANDER LEAVES, plus 2 tbsp for garnish

2 tbsp REDUCED-FAT SHREDDED MEXICAN CHEESE BLEND for garnish

1½ tbsp REDUCED-FAT SOUR CREAM for garnish

CONTINUED »

SKINNY DIPPERS: Baked Tortilla Chips, Roasted Fingerling Potatoes, baked potato chips

1. In a large nonstick frying pan over medium heat, warm the oil. Add the onion, garlic, and salt. Sauté, stirring frequently, until the onion is soft and light golden brown, about 12 minutes. Add the beef, chili powder, oregano, cumin, and cayenne. Continue to cook until the beef is browned, about 10 minutes. Add the tomato paste/tomato purée and continue to cook, stirring constantly, until all the liquid has evaporated, about 3 minutes. Add the broth and simmer until the broth is reduced to 2 tbsp. Add the tomatoes, including the juice from the can, and the water and sugar. Continue to simmer until the liquid is reduced by half. Add the beans and jalapeño and simmer for an additional 10 minutes. Stir in the lime juice, 3 tbsp green/spring onion, and 3 tbsp cilantro/fresh coriander. Taste and adjust the seasoning. Transfer to a warmed serving bowl.

2. To garnish, sprinkle the cheese over top, scatter the remaining green/spring onion and cilantro/fresh coriander on top, and add a dollop of sour cream in the center. Serve immediately.

DIP DO-AHEAD: This dip can be prepared 2 days in advance. Cover and refrigerate. Just before serving, heat until hot in a microwave or on the stovetop in a frying pan, and then garnish.

Not Your Mother's Deviled Ham Spread

Wait! Don't turn the page and pass up this recipe because you think this is a rendition of the deviled ham sold in paper-wrapped cans at the supermarket. This old classic is brought back into style when you start with deliciously smoked ham/gammon, add some fresh herbs and jalapeños, and flavor the mayonnaise base with Dijon mustard, freshly squeezed lemon juice, and a little hot sauce for an extra kick.

8 oz/225 g SMOKED HAM/GAMMON, roughly chopped

3 tbsp finely chopped FRESH FLAT-LEAF PARSLEY

1 JALAPEÑO CHILE, seeds and ribs removed (see page 16),
    finely minced

½ cup/120 ml REDUCED-FAT MAYONNAISE

2 tbsp REDUCED-FAT SOUR CREAM

1 tbsp DIJON MUSTARD

1 tbsp FRESH LEMON JUICE

½ tsp PAPRIKA

¼ tsp HOT SAUCE, such as Tabasco

SKINNY DIPPERS: Marbled Rye Toasts, Crostini, Baked Pita Chips,
Roasted Fingerling Potatoes, lavash

1. In the workbowl of a food processor fitted with the metal blade, pulse the ham/gammon until finely chopped. Transfer to a medium bowl and mix in the parsley and jalapeño.

2. In a small bowl, whisk together the mayonnaise, sour cream, mustard, lemon juice, paprika, and hot sauce until well combined. Using a rubber spatula, stir the mayonnaise mixture into the meat. Taste and adjust the seasoning. Transfer to a serving bowl and serve immediately.

DIP DO-AHEAD: This dip can be prepared up to 1 day in advance. Cover and refrigerate. Remove from the refrigerator 20 minutes before serving.

MAKES
about

2

cups
(480 ml)

SERVING SIZE

2

tbsp

CALORIES	47
FAT	3.1 g
SAT	0.7 g
MONO	0.3 g
POLY	0.1 g
PROTEIN	3 g
CARB	2 g
FIBER	0 g
CHOL	6 mg
IRON	0.2 mg
SODIUM	198 mg
CALC	5.5 mg

Skinny Shrimp Dip

Relish the splendors of beautifully pink, delicately cooked shrimp/
prawns when they're infused with the heady accents of ginger, garlic,
and green/spring onion. The sweet crustacean flavor is comple-
mented by a splash of sesame oil and just enough reduced-fat mayonnaise and sour cream to call this magical concoction a dip.

1 tsp KOSHER OR SEA SALT

1 lb/455 g medium UNCOOKED SHRIMP/PRAWNS in the shell

4 GREEN/SPRING ONIONS, including green tops, finely minced

1 rounded tbsp finely minced FRESH GINGER

1 tsp finely minced GARLIC

¼ cup/60 ml REDUCED-FAT MAYONNAISE

1½ tbsp REDUCED-FAT SOUR CREAM

4 tsp FRESH LEMON JUICE

1½ tsp ASIAN SESAME OIL

½ tsp FRESHLY GROUND WHITE PEPPER

SKINNY DIPPERS: Crostini, Baked Pita Chips, Baked Wonton Crisps,
Crudités, lavash

1. Fill a 3-qt/3-L saucepan two-thirds full of water, add ½ tsp
of the salt, and bring to a boil over high heat. Add the shrimp/
prawns and cook just until they are pink and firm, about 2 minutes.
Drain and rinse under cold water. Peel and devein the shrimp.
Finely chop the shrimp and transfer to a medium mixing bowl.

2. Mix the green/spring onions, ginger, garlic, and remaining
½ tsp salt with the shrimp. Add the mayonnaise, sour cream,
lemon juice, sesame oil, and pepper. Stir until the ingredients are
well combined. Transfer to a serving bowl. Cover and refrigerate
for at least 1 hour to allow the flavors to meld. Remove from the
refrigerator 20 minutes before serving.

DIP DO-AHEAD: This dip can be prepared up to 2 days in advance.
Cover and refrigerate.

MAKES about
3
cups (720 ml)

SERVING SIZE
2
tbsp

CALORIES	32
FAT	1.4 g
SAT	0.3 g
MONO	0.2 g
POLY	0.2 g
PROTEIN	4 g
CARB	1 g
FIBER	0 g
CHOL	38 mg
IRON	0.6 mg
SODIUM	111 mg
CALC	11 mg

MAKES
about

2

cups
(480 ml)

SERVING SIZE

2

tbsp

CALORIES   56
....
FAT   4.2 g
SAT   1.3 g
MONO   0.4 g
POLY   0.1 g
....
PROTEIN   3 g
CARB   2 g
FIBER   0 g
CHOL   14 mg
IRON   0.2 mg
SODIUM   121 mg
CALC   18 mg

Baked Crab Dip

Fresh crab meat is so rich, fabulous, and sweet that, for this dip, I wanted to highlight the texture and flavor of the crab without masking it. Served bubbly hot with a crisply browned, lemon zest–panko topping, this dip will be a party favorite—easy to put together, quick to bake, and quick to disappear, too.

6 oz/170 g FRESH CRABMEAT, well drained

1/2 cup/75 g diced RED BELL PEPPER/CAPSICUM

1/2 cup/25 g finely chopped FRESH FLAT-LEAF PARSLEY

3 tbsp snipped FRESH CHIVES

1/2 cup/120 ml REDUCED-FAT MAYONNAISE

4 oz/115 g WHIPPED CREAM CHEESE

1 1/2 tbsp FRESH LEMON JUICE

1/2 tsp HOT SAUCE, such as Tabasco

1/4 cup/20 g PANKO (Japanese bread crumbs)

1/2 tsp grated LEMON ZEST

SKINNY DIPPERS: Crostini, Baked Pita Chips, Baked Wonton Crisps, baked potato chips

1. Place the crabmeat in a medium bowl and flake with your fingers. Stir in the bell pepper/capsicum, parsley, and chives. Using a rubber spatula, gently stir in the mayonnaise, cream cheese, lemon juice, and hot sauce. Transfer to a 1-qt/1-L shallow baking dish. In a small bowl, combine the panko and lemon zest.

2. Position a rack in the upper third of the oven and preheat the oven to 425°F/220°C/gas 7. Just before baking, sprinkle the panko mixture on top and bake until the panko is toasty brown and the dip is bubbling at the edges, about 12 minutes. Serve hot.

DIP DO-AHEAD: The dip, without the panko topping, can be prepared, covered, and refrigerated up to 1 day in advance. Remove from the refrigerator 30 minutes before baking. The topping can be prepared up to 8 hours ahead and sprinkled on just before baking.

Italian Tuna & Caper Spread

MAKES
about

1¹/₃

cups
(315 ml)

SERVING SIZE

2

tbsp

CALORIES	50
FAT	3.2 g
SAT	0.6 g
MONO	0 g
POLY	0 g
PROTEIN	5 g
CARB	1 g
FIBER	0 g
CHOL	10 mg
IRON	0.2 mg
SODIUM	117 mg
CALC	5 mg

Canned tuna never had it so good. Combined with reduced-fat mayonnaise, whirled to a delicate smoothness and lightness, infused with a double hit of lemon, and speckled with capers and fresh herbs, tuna, a favorite pantry staple, makes an appealingly fresh, vibrant dip. I prefer to buy solid albacore tuna that has been hook-and-line caught and is dolphin safe. Mediterranean-style albacore tuna, packed in olive oil, has the most flavor.

1 can (6 oz/170 g) SOLID ALBACORE TUNA packed in olive oil

¹/₄ cup/60 ml REDUCED-FAT MAYONNAISE

1 tbsp grated LEMON ZEST

1¹/₂ tbsp FRESH LEMON JUICE

1 clove GARLIC, minced

¹/₂ tsp FRESHLY GROUND PEPPER

2 tbsp CAPERS, rinsed and blotted dry

2 tbsp minced FRESH FLAT-LEAF PARSLEY

1 tbsp minced FRESH OREGANO leaves

SKINNY DIPPERS: Marbled Rye Toasts, Crostini, Bruschetta, Baked Wonton Crisps, Baked Pita Chips, Crudités, Steamed Baby Artichokes, lavash

1. In the workbowl of a food processor fitted with the metal blade, process the tuna, including the oil from the can, with the mayonnaise, lemon zest and juice, garlic, and pepper. Process until smooth and creamy.

2. Transfer to a serving bowl and stir in the capers, parsley, and oregano. Taste and adjust the seasoning. Cover and refrigerate for 1 hour before serving to allow the flavors to meld. Serve chilled.

DIP DO-AHEAD: This dip can be prepared up to 2 days in advance. Cover and refrigerate until ready to serve.

CALORIES	54
FAT	4.1 g
SAT	2.2 g
MONO	1.2 g
POLY	0.3 g
PROTEIN	3 g
CARB	1 g
FIBER	0 g
CHOL	14 mg
IRON	0.1 mg
SODIUM	250 mg
CALC	25 mg

Smoked Salmon Pâté with Fresh Dill

Creamy pink salmon pâté, flecked with chives and dill, is a festive party hors d'oeuvre. I would be inclined to serve this pâté for a holiday gathering or New Year's Eve cocktail party. Since the pâté is made with reduced-fat cream cheese and sour cream, you save enough calories to justify a glass or two of Champagne!

5 oz/140 g LOW-FAT CREAM CHEESE (bar style), at room temperature

4 oz/115 g SMOKED SALMON (lox), chopped

¼ cup/60 ml REDUCED-FAT SOUR CREAM

1 tsp grated LEMON ZEST

1 tsp FRESH LEMON JUICE

Pinch of CAYENNE PEPPER

3 tbsp snipped FRESH CHIVES plus ½ tbsp for garnish

1 tsp minced FRESH DILL

SKINNY DIPPERS: Crostini, Marbled Rye Toasts, Baked Wonton Crisps, lavash

In the workbowl of a food processor fitted with the metal blade, combine the cream cheese, salmon, sour cream, lemon zest and juice, and cayenne to form a smooth paste. Transfer to a serving bowl and use a rubber spatula to blend in the 3 tbsp of the chives and the dill. Garnish with the remaining ½ tbsp of chives. Serve immediately.

DIP DO-AHEAD: The salmon pâté can be prepared up to 2 days in advance. Cover and refrigerate. Remove from the refrigerator 30 minutes before serving.

Poached Shrimp Dunk

I call this dish a "dunk" rather than a dip because the recipe doesn't include shrimp/prawns—the poached crustaceans are the skinny dippers meant to be dipped in the dunk! That last sentence might be a brain twister, but the real tongue pleaser is this luscious party dip. Poached shrimp/prawns make divine dippers, as do grilled asparagus and roasted fingerling potatoes. Use any leftovers as an accompaniment to grilled or broiled fish, particularly salmon or halibut.

1 cup/240 ml REDUCED-FAT MAYONNAISE

1 large HARD-COOKED EGG, finely chopped

3 tbsp finely chopped FRESH FENNEL, plus 2 tsp finely chopped
   FENNEL FRONDS

2 tbsp snipped FRESH CHIVES

1 tbsp FRESH LEMON JUICE

1 tsp peeled and grated FRESH GINGER

1 large clove GARLIC

1 tsp KOSHER OR SEA SALT

SKINNY DIPPERS: Poached Shrimp, Steamed Baby Artichokes, Grilled Asparagus, Roasted Fingerling Potatoes

1. In a medium bowl, mix together the mayonnaise, chopped egg, fennel and fennel fronds, chives, lemon juice, and ginger.

2. Finely chop the garlic and sprinkle with the salt. Using a chef's knife, press the flat side of the blade back and forth across the garlic to make a paste. Transfer it to the bowl with the mayonnaise mixture and stir until well combined. Transfer the dip to a serving bowl. Cover and refrigerate for 2 hours before serving to allow the flavors to meld. Serve chilled.

DIP DO-AHEAD: This dip can be prepared up to 2 days in advance. Cover and refrigerate until ready to serve.

MAKES

1⅓

cups
(315 ml)

SERVING SIZE

2

tbsp

CALORIES	77
FAT	7.2 g
SAT	1.2 g
MONO	0.2 g
POLY	0.1 g
PROTEIN	1 g
CARB	2 g
FIBER	0 g
CHOL	26 mg
IRON	0.1 mg
SODIUM	275 mg
CALC	5 mg

6

Crudités and Other Skinny Dippers

The appeal of dippers comes from the contrast in texture—the big-chip crunch of baked bagel chips coated with a creamy hummus, the "pow!" of crispness from garlic-grilled bruschetta topped with chunky tapenade, the snap of garden-fresh crudités slicked with a Svelte Green Goddess Dip. This chapter is filled with slimmed-down dippers ready to party with a book full of dips. These mouth-watering bites arrive hot off the grill, warm from the oven, blanched and beautiful, or simply raw and ready to fill a platter, basket, or bowl. It's a healthful crunchfest here!

Crudités

Now, here is a big category of healthful and calorie-conscious dippers—raw and blanched vegetables, which are collectively known as crudités. Munch away! The veggies in this long list are a treasure trove of nutritional goodness, packed with farm-fresh flavor, antioxidants, vitamins, minerals, and fiber.

Along with all the crunchy chips that typically appear on party tables, a platter or basket filled with a variety of vegetables makes a show-stopping centerpiece for an assortment of dips. The best way to assemble crudités for presentation is to think about which vegetables are in season and which will taste best with the dips you are serving. Then artfully select an assortment that will bring different colors and textures to the platter.

Instead of listing the vegetables in alphabetical order, I've arranged them in two categories: "Raw Veggies Ready to Eat" don't need to be cooked before they are served, only prepped, cut, and arranged; "Veggies to Blanch and Steam" taste and look better when partially cooked. Blanching brings out the natural sweetness of certain vegetables, leaves them crisp while softening the crunch, and gives green veggies a vibrant hue. Steaming preserves flavor and vitamins.

CRUDITÉS DO-AHEAD: Unless otherwise noted, the vegetables can be prepared 1 day in advance, wrapped in damp paper towels/absorbent paper, and stored in a lock-top plastic bag in the refrigerator.

Raw Veggies Ready to Eat

BELGIAN ENDIVE/CHICORY: Trim the bases, carefully separate the heads into leaves, and rinse the leaves and pat them dry.

BELL PEPPERS/CAPSICUMS: Use red, yellow, or orange bell peppers/capsicums. (I'm not a big fan of the green variety for crudités. They have an acidic aftertaste that doesn't work well with dips.) To prepare, cut them in half lengthwise and remove the cores, seeds, and ribs. Cut lengthwise into long strips about ¾ in/2 cm wide.

CARROTS: Use whole "baby-cut" carrots sold ready to eat, or buy medium carrots and cut them into strips 3 in/7.5 cm long. Petite carrots, with their feathery tops, look terrific on a crudité platter; just peel the carrots, leaving 1 in/2.5 cm of the green tops on.

CELERY: Trim the tops and bottoms of the celery ribs, but leave the leafy tops on the tender inner ribs. Use a vegetable peeler to peel the strings from the back of the larger ribs. Cut the ribs in half lengthwise and then cut them crosswise into strips 3 in/7.5 cm long. As an alternative, the stalks can be cut crosswise on a sharp diagonal into slices 1 in/2.5 cm wide.

CHERRY TOMATOES: Use the larger, classic cherry tomatoes, as they are easier to pick up and dip. Leave the stems attached for a pretty presentation.

CUCUMBERS: If using seedless English/hothouse cucumbers, leave the skin on and trim the ends. Cut the cucumbers length-wise into quarters and then cut them crosswise into "fingers" 3 in/7.5 cm long. As an alternative, cut the cucumber crosswise on a sharp diagonal into slices ¼ in/6 mm thick. If using regular cucumbers, trim the ends, peel the cucumbers, and then cut them in half lengthwise. Remove the seeds using a melon baller or a teaspoon and cut them into 3-in/7.5-cm fingers.

FENNEL BULB: Cut off the fronds and stalks, if still attached. Cut the bulb in half lengthwise and use a paring knife to remove the core from each half. Cut the fennel into wide wedges, separating the layers.

GREEN/SPRING ONIONS: Trim the root end, leaving the onions whole, but trim some of the green tops so that the finished onions are about 4 in/10 cm long.

JICAMA: Cut the jicama into quarters, if whole. Using a paring knife (not a vegetable peeler), peel the jicama by placing the blade just under the skin and then pulling the peel away in one whole piece. Cut the jicama into strips that are about 3 in/7.5 cm long and ½ in/12 mm thick.

CONTINUED »

LETTUCE: The leaves from the hearts of romaine/Cos lettuce are attractive on a crudité platter, as are wedges of butter/Boston lettuce. Thin wedges of iceberg lettuce can also give a great crunch.

RADISHES: Buy bunched radishes with their tops on rather than the packaged, trimmed radishes sold in a cello bag. Trim the root ends; for an attractive presentation, leave on about 1 in/2.5 cm of the green tops and some of the freshest leaves. Wrap the prepared radishes in damp paper towels/absorbent paper and store in a lock-top plastic bag in the refrigerator for up to 1 day.

SUMMER SQUASH: Zucchini/courgettes and other summer squash, especially miniature squash such as pattypan, taste and look terrific on a crudité platter. For the miniatures, trim the tops and leave them whole. For standard-size squash, trim the ends, cut into 3-in/7.5-cm lengths, and then cut lengthwise into $\frac{1}{2}$-in/12-mm wedges. As an alternative, the squash can be cut crosswise on a sharp diagonal into slices $\frac{1}{4}$ in/6 mm wide.

Veggies to Blanch and Steam

BLANCHING: Blanching vegetables involves nothing more than plunging them into a large pot of boiling salted water, cooking the vegetables briefly, refreshing them in a large bowl of ice water, and then blotting them dry with paper towels/absorbent paper or lint-free cotton towels. The vegetables lose their raw taste and, in the case of green vegetables, turn a brilliant green, making them quite attractive on a crudité platter. Blanching greatly improves the taste of the vegetables listed in this category. Approximate cooking times are given for each vegetable. If you are blanching an assortment of vegetables, you can cook them in batches in the same pot of water, but start with the ones with the mildest flavors, such as carrots, then cook more pungent vegetables such as cauliflower and broccoli at the end.

CONTINUED »

To blanch vegetables, fill a large pot three-fourths full of water. Bring to a boil over high heat and add 2 tbsp of kosher or sea salt. Have ready a large bowl of ice water and a pair of tongs, a mesh strainer, or a large slotted spoon to quickly remove the vegetables after blanching. Have several layers of paper towels/absorbent paper laid out on a counter for draining the vegetables. Roll them up in several thicknesses of dry paper and store them in a lock-top plastic bag in the refrigerator for up to 1 day.

STEAMING: All the vegetables listed in this section can also be steamed— with longer cooking times than blanching.

ASPARAGUS: Use medium-size asparagus (pencil-thin asparagus flop over and are hard to dip) and trim the woody bases to a uniform length. Peel the stems. Cook until bright green and crisp-tender, about 2 minutes.

BROCCOLI: Cut the broccoli into bite-size florets. If desired, trim and peel the stems, then cut the stems crosswise on a sharp diagonal into slices ¼ in/ 6 mm thick. Cook until bright green and crisp-tender, 1½ to 2 minutes.

CARROTS: Carrot sticks and petite whole carrots can be blanched, if desired (see page 123 for preparation). Cook until crisp-tender, about 2 minutes.

CAULIFLOWER: Remove all outer leaves. Cut the cauliflower into bite-size florets. Cook until crisp-tender, about 2 minutes.

GREEN BEANS: Trim the stem end only. Cook the beans until bright green and crisp-tender, about 2 minutes.

SNOW PEAS/MANGETOUTS AND SUGAR SNAP PEAS: Trim the stem end of each pea and remove the string along the bottom. Cook the peas until bright green and crisp-tender, about 1 minute.

Roasted Cauliflower or Fingerling Potatoes

Roasting vegetables—cauliflower and potatoes in particular—is a terrific way to enhance their flavor without adding a lot of fat. The vegetables, when slicked with a small amount of oil and a sprinkling of salt, caramelize in the oven, especially the edges placed cut-side down on the baking sheet/tray. Roasted veggies make terrific dippers, and the recipe couldn't be easier—cut, toss, and bake.

---

1 head CAULIFLOWER, outer leaves removed, and cut into
    bite-size florets

    or

15 large FINGERLING POTATOES, halved lengthwise

2 tbsp EXTRA-VIRGIN OLIVE OIL

KOSHER OR SEA SALT

---

1. Position a rack in the center of the oven and preheat the oven to 400°F/200°C/gas 6. Have ready a large, rimmed baking sheet/tray.

2. In a large bowl, toss the cauliflower or potatoes with the olive oil. Sprinkle lightly with salt.

3. If roasting cauliflower, arrange the florets with one cut side down in a single layer on the baking sheet/tray. If roasting potatoes, arrange them cut-side down in a single layer on the baking sheet/tray.

4. Bake until the vegetables are tender when pierced with a knife and the cut sides are caramelized, 25 to 35 minutes. Let cool in the pan for 10 minutes. Arrange on a serving platter. Serve warm or at room temperature.

DIPPER DO-AHEAD: The roasted vegetables can be prepared up to 8 hours in advance. Cover and set aside at room temperature. Warm just before serving, if desired.

MAKES
about

20

cauliflower florets

OR

30

potato halves

SERVING SIZE

2

florets

OR

2

potato halves

MAKES

24
asparagus spears

OR

16
eggplant halves

SERVING SIZE

2
spears

OR

1
eggplant half

Grilled Asparagus or Japanese Eggplant

Vegetables are transformed on the grill. Their colors brighten, their flavors intensify, and their exteriors crisp while their interiors soften. Grilled asparagus or halved Japanese eggplants/aubergines make ideal dippers because they are crisp-tender when grilled, yet sturdy enough to dip.

24 thick ASPARAGUS SPEARS

or

8 JAPANESE EGGPLANTS/AUBERGINES, stem end trimmed, halved lengthwise

EXTRA-VIRGIN OLIVE OIL

KOSHER OR SEA SALT

1. Prepare a hot fire in a charcoal grill/barbecue, preheat a gas grill/barbecue on high, or use a stovetop grill pan.

2. For the asparagus, snap off the fibrous bottom end of each spear, or trim the whole bunch to a uniform length. Place the spears in a baking dish, toss with olive oil, and season with salt. For the eggplants/aubergines, brush on all sides with a little olive oil. Sprinkle the cut sides lightly with salt.

3. Oil the grill grate. Place the vegetables directly over the hot fire (or in a heated grill pan slicked lightly with oil) and cook, turning as needed, until grill marks appear on all sides and the vegetables are crisp-tender, about 4 minutes (the timing will vary depending on the thickness of the vegetables). Transfer to a warmed platter. Serve immediately at room temperature.

DIPPER DO-AHEAD: The grilled vegetables can be prepared up to 8 hours in advance. Arrange the asparagus or eggplant halves on a wire rack set over a baking sheet/tray and set aside, loosely covered, at room temperature. If desired, warm the vegetables in an oven preheated to 300°F/150°C/gas 2 just before serving.

Steamed Baby Artichokes

MAKES

24

artichokes

SERVING SIZE

1

artichoke

Artichokes always taste waterlogged to me when they are cooked in boiling water.

2 LEMONS

24 small (baby) ARTICHOKES

1. Fill a large bowl two-thirds full of cold water. Cut the lemons in half and squeeze the juice into the water. Drop the squeezed halves into the water as well. Set the bowl within close reach. Working quickly, with one artichoke at a time, trim the bottom of the artichoke flat or, if there is a stem, use a paring knife to pare off the tough green fibers and leave the stem intact. Pull back and tear off the dark green leaves until you reach the tender, yellowish green ones. Cut crosswise to trim off the green pointy tips, about 1/2 in/6 mm from the top of the artichoke. If any tough outer pieces of leaf remain near the stem end, trim those. Drop the artichoke in the bowl of lemon water to keep it from discoloring. Continue until all artichokes are trimmed.

2. Have ready a steamer rack and a pan of simmering water. Drain the artichokes and arrange them on the steamer rack. Place the rack over the water, making sure the water is 1 in/2.5 cm or so below the rack. Cover the pan with a tight-fitting lid and steam the artichokes until tender, when a paring knife slides easily through the heart of the artichoke, 8 to 10 minutes. Use a slotted spoon or tongs to transfer the artichokes to a plate and let them cool to room temperature. Cut the artichokes in half lengthwise before serving.

DIPPER DO-AHEAD: The artichokes can be prepared up to 1 day in advance. Once cooled, cover and refrigerate. Remove from the refrigerator 45 minutes before serving.

Bruschetta

The word *bruschetta* comes from the Italian word *bruscare*, meaning "to roast over coals." A specialty of Rome, this traditional garlic bread is made by rubbing slices of good, coarse crusty bread with fresh garlic and then drizzling the bread with extra-virgin olive oil. The bread is then grilled/barbecued or broiled/grilled. To make the bruschetta a bit lighter, calorie-wise, I lightly spray the slices with extra-virgin olive oil spray. High-quality ingredients are the key here. Buy crusty artisanal bread, either a baguette or a large round loaf. Grill the bread so it is just crisp on the outside but still soft on the inside. Otherwise, with the first bite the bruschetta shatters, making the remainder inelegant to eat.

1 loaf RUSTIC BREAD

EXTRA-VIRGIN OLIVE OIL SPRAY

2 or 3 cloves GARLIC

KOSHER OR SEA SALT

1. TO GRILL/BARBECUE THE BRUSCHETTA, preheat a gas grill/barbecue on medium, or prepare a charcoal fire and wait until the coals reach the white-ash stage and the fire begins to die down to low coals.

TO BROIL/GRILL THE BRUSCHETTA, adjust the oven rack so it is about 4 in/10 cm from the heat source and preheat the broiler/grill.

2. Cut the bread on the diagonal into thick slices. If using a round loaf, cut each slice in half or even in thirds to make appetizer-size portions. Spray both sides lightly with olive oil.

3. Cook the bread until nicely browned on both sides but still soft within, being careful not to burn it. As soon as the bread comes off the heat, rub one or both sides with the garlic, depending on how much garlic flavor you like. Sprinkle the bread very lightly with salt. Serve the bread hot, warm, or at room temperature.

DIPPER DO-AHEAD: The bruschetta are best made shortly before serving, but can be prepared 2 hours ahead and stored uncovered at room temperature.

Crostini

Crostini means "little toasts" in Italian. They are small, thin slices of toasted bread, usually brushed with olive oil and baked. To make crostini "skinnier," I give them a wisp of extra flavor by misting them with extra-virgin olive oil spray. If you want plain toasts to serve with dips, simply omit the oil.

1 BAGUETTE, about 1½ in/4 cm in diameter

EXTRA-VIRGIN OLIVE OIL SPRAY

1. Position one rack in the center of the oven and a second rack in the upper third; preheat to 350°F/180°C/gas 4.

2. Cut the baguette into slices ⅓ in/8 mm thick and arrange in a single layer on two baking sheets/trays. Spray lightly on both sides with olive oil. Bake until lightly browned on top, about 7 minutes. Turn the slices and switch the positions of the baking sheets. Bake until the crostini are lightly browned on the second side, about 5 minutes longer. They should be crunchy but not brittle. Serve warm or at room temperature.

DIPPER DO-AHEAD: The crostini can be made up to 3 days in advance. Store in a lock-top plastic bag or in an airtight container at room temperature.

Herbed Cheddar Cheese Straws

Though puff pastry, per se, is not a low-calorie dough, it can be eaten in moderation and used to make thin breadsticks. These cheese straws make great dippers—crunchy, big-flavored, and fun to eat. Double the recipe for a crowd—the straws will be gone before you know it!

1 sheet FROZEN PUFF PASTRY DOUGH (from a 17.3-oz/490-g package)

1 cup/115 g shredded REDUCED-FAT CHEDDAR CHEESE

1 tbsp snipped FRESH CHIVES

1 tsp minced FRESH THYME

¾ tsp PIMENTÓN (Spanish smoked paprika)

¼ tsp CAYENNE PEPPER

ALL-PURPOSE/PLAIN FLOUR for dusting

1 EGG, beaten with 2 tsp water

1. Let the pastry sheet thaw at room temperature for 30 minutes. (Tightly seal the remaining pastry in the package and freeze for another use.)

2. Position one rack in the center of the oven and a second rack in the lower third and preheat to 425°F/220°C/gas 7. Have ready two rimmed baking sheets/trays, preferably nonstick. Line pans that do not have a nonstick finish with parchment paper/baking paper or use Silpat mats.

3. In a small bowl, mix together the cheese, chives, thyme, pimentón, and cayenne. Set aside.

CONTINUED »

4. Unfold the pastry sheet and place it on a lightly floured cutting board. If there are any cracks in the pastry, gently pinch them closed. Using a lightly floured rolling pin, first roll over the pastry gently, just enough to remove the fold marks, and then roll it out into a 10-by-15-in/25-by-38-cm rectangle. Cut in half lengthwise to form two 5-by-15-in/12-by-38-cm rectangles. Brush each piece with the egg wash. Arrange one piece of the dough with the long side facing you and distribute the cheese filling evenly over it. Place the second piece of dough, egg-wash-side down, on top of the cheese, lining up the edges evenly. Using the rolling pin, press the sheets together to secure the cheese firmly between the layers, especially at the edges.

5. Using a sharp knife or pizza wheel, cut the filled and pressed pastry crosswise into 30 strips, each ½ in/12 mm wide. Working with one strip at a time, twist the cheese straw three times and lay it on a baking sheet/tray, pressing down the ends firmly to keep it from untwisting during baking. Continue to twist and arrange the remaining strips, placing them 1 in/2.5 cm apart on the baking sheets.

6. Bake for 8 minutes, switch the positions of the baking sheets, and continue to bake until the cheese straws are puffed, golden brown, and crisp, 4 to 6 minutes longer. Transfer to a wire rack and let cool slightly. Serve warm or at room temperature.

DIPPER DO-AHEAD: The cheese straws can be made up to 3 days in advance. Store in a lock-top plastic bag or in an airtight container at room temperature. The day of serving, arrange the cheese straws on a rimmed baking sheet/tray and crisp them for 7 to 10 minutes in a preheated 375°F/190°C/gas 5 oven.

Baked Pita Chips

MAKES

80

chips

SERVING SIZE

3

chips

Baked properly, these chips are almost irresistible. Plain and seasoned pita chips are so easy to make and so crunchy good that a batch will be gone before you know it.

5 PITA BREADS, white or whole-wheat, or a combination

1. Position one rack in the center of the oven and a second rack in the upper third, and preheat to 350°F/180°C/gas 4.

2. Using a knife or your fingers, split each pita bread horizontally in half along the outer edges to form two rounds. Cut each round into eight wedges. Distribute the wedges in a single layer on two rimmed baking sheets/trays. Don't crowd the pita wedges; it is better to bake them in two batches. Bake until lightly browned and crisp, 10 to 12 minutes, turning the crisps over halfway through the baking time. Let cool. Serve at room temperature.

DIPPER DO-AHEAD: These chips can be prepared up to 5 days in advance and stored in a covered container at room temperature.

Variations

PARMESAN-CRUSTED PITA CHIPS: Before cutting the pita breads into eighths, brush with olive oil and sprinkle generously with freshly grated Parmesan cheese. Cut the pitas into wedges and bake as directed.

LEMON OLIVE OIL AND FRESH THYME PITA CHIPS: Before cutting the pita breads into eighths, brush with lemon-infused olive oil and sprinkle lightly with minced fresh thyme. Cut the pitas into wedges and bake as directed.

SPICE-COATED PITA CHIPS: In a small bowl, mix together 3 tbsp extra-virgin olive oil, 1¼ tsp ground cumin, and 1¼ tsp chili powder. Before cutting the pita breads into eighths, brush with the olive oil mixture. Cut the pitas into wedges and bake as directed.

Baked Bagel Chips

MAKES
about

64
bagel chips

SERVING SIZE

3
chips

There is no comparison between store-bought and homemade bagel chips. Homemade bagel chips are so good—addictively so—that I avoid making them unless company is coming, because I'll eat the whole batch. Plus, they are so simple to make. I love all the possible variations: Try using rye, herbed, sesame, garlic, onion, or multigrain bagels.

4 BAGELS

EXTRA-VIRGIN OLIVE OIL for brushing bagels

1. Position one rack in the center of the oven and a second rack in the upper third and preheat to 325°F/165°C/gas 3. Line two baking sheets/trays with parchment paper/baking paper.

2. With a sharp bread knife, cut the bagels in half crosswise to form two short horseshoes. Stand the bagel halves on their cut sides and carefully slice them as thinly as possible, getting about 8 slices out of each half. Arrange the slices in a single layer on the baking sheets. Brush both sides of the bagels very lightly with olive oil. Bake until lightly brown on one side, 5 to 7 minutes. Turn the slices over and switch the positions of the baking sheets/trays. Bake until lightly brown and crisp on the other side, about 2 minutes longer. Arrange on a serving platter or in a basket and serve warm or at room temperature.

DIPPER DO-AHEAD: The bagel chips are best served within 8 hours of making them, but can be prepared 2 days in advance and stored in a covered container at room temperature. The chips will soften if stored in plastic bags.

Variation

....

ROASTED GARLIC BAGEL CHIPS: Use garlic bagels and brush the bagel slices with roasted-garlic olive oil. Bake as directed.

Baked Wonton Crisps

Explosively crunchy wonton crisps are astonishingly good—and a snap to make. They go well with so many of these dips, but a couple of my favorite pairings are with the Skinny Shrimp Dip (page 111) and the Baked Crab Dip (page 112).

When buying wonton wrappers to bake, choose thin wrappers over thick ones. Thin wonton wrappers will yield a better crunch. They usually come 100 to a package; you can freeze any unused squares, first wrapping them in plastic wrap/cling film and then sealing them in a lock-top plastic bag. Thaw them in the refrigerator before using.

30 (3-by-3½-in/7.5-by-9-cm) thin square WONTON WRAPPERS

1 tbsp ASIAN SESAME OIL

KOSHER OR SEA SALT

1. Position one rack in the center of the oven and a second rack in the upper third and preheat to 425°F/220°C/gas 7.

2. Using a sharp knife, cut the wonton squares diagonally in half to form two triangles. Alternatively, use a cookie cutter, such as a flower- or star-shaped one, to cut the wrappers.

3. Using a pastry brush, lightly brush two rimmed baking sheets/ trays with half of the sesame oil. Arrange the wonton wrappers, close together but not touching, in a single layer on the baking sheets. Brush the top side of the dough with the remaining oil. Sprinkle very lightly with salt. Bake the wonton wrappers for 3 minutes. Switch the positions of the baking sheets/trays and continue baking the crisps until they are speckled brown and crunchy, about 2 minutes longer. (Watch carefully so they don't overbake and brown completely.) Let cool on the baking sheets/ trays. Transfer to a basket or serving bowl and set aside until ready to serve.

DIPPER DO-AHEAD: Wonton crisps are best served within 8 hours of making them, but can be prepared 1 day in advance and stored in a covered container at room temperature. The baked crisps will soften if stored in plastic bags.

Baked Tortilla Chips

Crisp and full of flavor, these crunchy triangles, warm from the oven, will turn any party into a fiesta.

MAKES
about

96

tortilla chips

SERVING SIZE

3

chips

12 (6- to 8-in/15- to 20-cm) white or yellow CORN TORTILLAS

CANOLA OIL for brushing

KOSHER OR SEA SALT

1. Position one rack in the center of the oven and a second rack in the upper third and preheat to 400°F/200°C/gas 6.

2. Lightly brush the tortillas on both sides with canola oil. Cut the tortillas into 6 or 8 wedges. Arrange the wedges on two rimmed baking sheets/trays in a single layer without crowding. (Bake the tortilla chips in batches if they won't all fit.) Bake the tortillas on one side for 5 minutes and then turn the chips over. Switch the positions of the baking sheets/trays and bake until crisp and just beginning to color, about 5 minutes longer. Sprinkle lightly with salt, and transfer to a serving bowl.

DIPPER DO-AHEAD: The tortilla chips are best served within 8 hours of making them. Store uncovered at room temperature and rewarm in the oven just before serving.

Variations

SEEDED TORTILLA CHIPS: In a small bowl, combine $1/3$ cup/ 75 ml canola oil with 4 tsp ground coriander, 2 tsp kosher salt, and $1\frac{1}{2}$ tbsp each of poppy seeds and sesame seeds. Mix well to combine. Generously brush this mixture on one side of each of the tortillas and then cut the tortillas into wedges and bake as directed.

CHILE-LIME TORTILLA CHIPS: Combine $1/4$ cup/60 ml canola oil with 2 tbsp fresh lime juice, $1/2$ tsp each of ground coriander, ground cumin, and salt, plus 1 tsp paprika and 1 tsp chili powder. Mix well to combine. Brush on one side of the tortillas and cut them into wedges. Bake as directed.

Marbled Rye Toasts

I much prefer homemade rye toasts to the imported, packaged rye crisps. Plus, for parties, you can mix and match the varieties of rye bread you buy, offering a basket filled with marbled rye toasts alongside others made from dark rye or even Swedish rye. This recipe would work well with small loaves of party rye, too.

12 slices marbled or dark RYE BREAD

EXTRA-VIRGIN OLIVE OIL SPRAY

KOSHER OR SEA SALT

1. Position one rack in the center of the oven and a second rack in the upper third and preheat to 425°F/220°C/gas 7.

2. From each slice of bread, cut two rectangles, each approximately 2 by 2½ in/5 by 6 cm. Arrange in a single layer on two baking sheets/trays. Spray lightly on both sides with olive oil. Sprinkle lightly on one side with salt. Bake until lightly crisped on top, about 5 minutes. Turn the slices and switch the positions of the baking sheets/trays. Bake until the rye bread is crisp on the second side, about 5 minutes longer. They should be crunchy but not brittle. Serve warm or at room temperature.

DIPPER DO-AHEAD: The rye toasts can be made up to 2 days in advance. Store in an airtight container at room temperature.

Poached Shrimp

Sweet-tasting Gulf shrimp/prawns (preferably wild-caught) turn a beautiful pink hue after a gentle poaching in a citrus-and-spice-infused bath. Their delicate flavor is enhanced when they are cooked in their shells. That being said, if you are pressed for time, go ahead and buy them peeled and deveined raw, then follow these same cooking directions.

MAKES
about

50
poached shrimp

SERVING SIZE

3
shrimp

½ LEMON, cut into thin slices

1 BAY LEAF

10 PEPPERCORNS

1¾ tsp KOSHER OR SEA SALT

1½ lb/680 g medium (31 to 35 count) UNCOOKED SHRIMP/PRAWNS in the shell

In a medium saucepan, combine the lemon slices, bay leaf, peppercorns, and salt. Add 5 cups/1.2 L of cold water and bring to a boil over high heat. Simmer for 5 minutes. Reduce the heat to medium-low and add the shrimp/prawns. Cook just until they are pink and cooked through, about 3 minutes. Drain in a colander and rinse under cold water, discarding the lemon slices and any spices clinging to the shellfish. Peel and devein the shrimp/prawns. Arrange on a platter and serve immediately, or transfer to a covered container and refrigerate until ready to serve.

DIPPER DO-AHEAD: The dish can be prepared up to 1 day in advance. Cover and refrigerate.

Index

141